Yoga Katha
Yoga Sutras,
by trip aum santi

Aum Shanti
http://seva.life

Ordering Information:
Quantity sales. Special discounts are available on quantity purchases by corporations, associations, and others. For details, contact the publisher at the address above.

Printed in the United States of America

First Printing, 2018

ISBN: 9781521097892

Dedication

There is no possible way I could properly thank everyone who helped me develop this book, but I will try.

First and foremost, I would like to thank my endlessly, loving wife, Morgaine. She set up a home inside my consciousness and opened up all the windows to let the light in. Without her, this book would never have been written.

I would like to thank the lotus feet of my dear teacher Adam Sobel and his family. For over a decade, they have shown me the paper walls of my awareness, and how easy it is to step through them; to become vegan, to understand selfless service, and find God.

I'd like to thank the sadhus I have become dear friends with. Dhanurdhara Swami, Swami Atmananda Udasin, Sri Vishnu the begger from the Ganga River. They are the living, breathing evidence of a love so pure, nothing else is necessary but to practice.

And no dedication would ever be complete without offering my gratitude to everyone who has saved my life -- specifically, my mother.

Introduction

About the Author

This particular life began when I started hitch hiking as a teenager. This novelty of living in the moment led me to living on the street for a few years, criss-crossing the United States, squatting in abandoned buildings, caves, mountain tops, and eventually in an endangered old growth redwood tree.

Then one day I was in India. I studied under the tutelage of Sri Dhanurdhara Swami, chanting sun up to sun down, and through my sleep. The mantra followed me through my abhyasa in ashtanga yoga as taught by Sri Pattabhi Jois. These two practices, combined, dissolved me. Something in me began to quiet like I had never experienced before.

One day, I wasn't me. There was the breeze, a passing bird, and the continuum of love that holds this life we share together. I was no longer while the world was. And though nothing had changed, everything was different.

It's an experience that I found described by Sri Patanjali, the author of the Yoga Sutras which was written more than 2000 years ago. And so with a humble heart, I dedicated now two and a half years of my life to writing this book.

Translations

Every generation carries its own voice. It's own pressures, and fears design a language for the children of that era. The Yoga Sutras never cease to be relevant because they're so simple. But it's their simplicity that is very easy to overlook. From hundreds of dialogues I've had with other practitioners, to watching the popularity of yoga explode over the past decade, I realized there was a gap in our culture's philosophical understanding of Eastern thought.

A gap caused by magical descriptions of yogis in an otherwise grounded and critical mellinial people. As such, people generally skip the third and fourth chapters of the Yoga Sutras.

But Patanjali didn't author a book on acrobatics and magical flight, he authored a book on awareness. Things like levitation, shapeshifting, and immortality become rational when the context is our consciousness and not our bodies. It was a commentary I felt pressured to write because I have yet to, as of writing this, find one I felt was accessible to my living era.

I carefully studied the book, the Yoga Sutras, its Sanskrit, and every single translation of it available from Vyasa, Vijnana Bikshu, Vacaspati Misra, Edwin Bryant, B. K. S. Iyenger, Swami Satchidinanda, to any dusty run off copy in bookstores throughout India. For hours on end, every day, I compared translations, and muled over various Sanskrit dictionaries and resources to find the humble words in this book today.

My objective was to make the philosophy accessible and simple. In some cases, I heavily simplified the verse in order to accomplish this. My goal being not to distract the reader by lists of particular ailments. For example in 1.30, instead of listing every individual example of distraction, I'd rather the reader dwell in the idea of distraction by itself. However, I did leave the original Sanskrit available for readers to assume their own judgement.

My translations are by no means definitive. Take them as you want. And pass them on as you want. I thank you so sincerely for reading.

Yoga Katha
Yoga Sutras

Table of Contents

Chapter One

Text 1.1

Practice of yoga is now.

अथ योगानुशासनम्

atha yoga-anuśāsanam

atha	And so, now
yoga	Origin, oneness, eternal truth
anuśāsanam	Continuation of instruction

And so, continuing on what you know of yoga, this teaching of yoga is presented.

Every origin is yet a ripple among many, and rarely the first. The teachings of yoga have no beginning. Patanjali knew this. This is why he wrote this first line with the word for teachings, *śāsanam* with the prefix, *anu*. Using the word *anu* infers that this teaching continues an existing teaching. It is simply yet another ripple from a stone thrown a long time ago. Long before the Yoga Sutras were produced and spread throughout Asia and the Middle East and copied into over forty different languages by the 12th century. The Yoga Sutras are about *yoga* which means yolk or union. Yoga can be considered the science of origin.

It asks — what was that rock thrown that caused the ripple? Where did the teaching come from? Where does all teaching come from? Where did your consciousness come from?

Going back to the source - in now

Yoga is the art of retracing our steps backwards, back to the very beginning, and becoming one with that origin. Through its meditation and asana, we are following the footprints of our identity back to the source. We follow our fears, passions, and habits all back to a common origin. And it is from this beginning that we find the clearest context of life. From here, we can observe the rise and fall of every kingdom, every heartbreak, and the unyielding sincerity of love. In the same way climbing a mountain gives one a higher context of the path they tread. Following our consciousness to the root of its perception gives one a higher context to the nature of existence. This book will show you how.

yoga is witnessing the modifications of the mind

Text 1.2

योगश्चित्तवृत्तिनिरोधः

yogaś-citta-vr̥tti-nirodhaḥ

yogaḥ	Yoga
citta	Thoughts, that which is changeable
vr̥tti	A fluctuation of the mind
nirodhaḥ	To control, to let be

Yoga is the purification of consciousness and its manifestations.

Many translations suggest that *nirodhah* is control, or restraint against our thought processes. But a better word is allowance because our purest state of mind is as natural as a flower finding its way through a crack in the sidewalk. This flower knows exactly what to do. It's not restraining or controlling itself in the least. It's simply performing its nature to grow and flower. Just as our highest sense of conscious awareness knows exactly what to do. All we have to do is stop developing a concrete jungle on this fertile Earth.

The only thing that requires effort is the act of stopping our consciousness from awakening. Things like self-desire, cravings for power, cravings for attention, or the insatiable thirst for more and more and more — this is the concrete blocking your wildflower's destiny. I've witnessed people put so much effort into justified and beautifully sculpted walls around their lives. Walls that give rise to the multiplicity of their fears and anxieties. They essentially complain of how difficult their life is while they cement out the sun.

The yoga practice is the art of making no effort, and instead allowing nature to reclaim whatever walls were built. Just as a city if left unattended will eventually be devoured by a flowering forest in matrimony. Nature knows exactly what to do. It's always waiting. Just as your spirit has always been waiting. This idea of a you simply has to stop getting in the way. And this initial letting go may require effort, but the absolute expression of letting go is and will always be effortless. This is yoga.

Then the seer abides in its true self.

Text 1.3

तदा द्रष्टुः स्वरूपेऽवस्थानम्
tadā draṣṭuḥ svarūpe-'vasthānam

tadā	Then
draṣṭuḥ	The true seer
svarūpe	In its own essential form
avasthānam	Abiding in, rest within, recognize

When yoga is accomplished, you will have insight of our true nature.

Our perception is an incredible piece of architecture. To understand it, we must swim upstream to the origin of this perceiver, to the original seer. That is, to look so far inward before the phenomenon of sense, before the phenomenon of mind, before the phenomenon of intelligence, before reason or discrimination, and especially before the phenomenon of Self.

It is here, that consciousness is universal, experiencing itself through all matter, all beings, inanimate, and imagined. In this state, nothing is having a unique experience from something else. It is consciousness perceiving itself through itself. The world we envision, the world we taste and smell, the music we listen to, our myriad of thoughts — are all mere shadows of this eternal experience.

Everything we perceive is an echo of a greater perception that existed long before us and will continue to exist long after our body perishes. The practice of yoga is withdrawing the locus of our perception to this natural beginning. Instead of seeing the context of your life by your hunger or fears or instincts, yoga withdraws the context of your life to the beginning of all life. All existence. The very root of nature itself.

It is from this place, we make our clearest and greatest decisions. This is because our choices are not laced with fear or materialism or biological mechanics. Instead, we move and interact with the world at the height of pure consciousness. Also known as enlightenment. Also known as God consciousness. But here, Patanjali defines it as existing within your own true nature.

Text 1.4

वृत्ति सारूप्यमितरत्र
vr̥tti sārūpyam-itaratra

vr̥tti	Thought waves, fluctuations
sārūpyam	Mirrored, identified
itaratra	Otherwise, at other times

Otherwise, thoughts take on the form of the world around us, harden like clay, and presume that they are you.

Thoughts are as superfluous as the rain. Just because rain falls on us, doesn't mean we are the rain. Just as we are not our memories. We are not our ideas. We simply project a self among these random phenomena and pretend that we are them. Just as a wave can, for just a moment, separate itself from the ocean and claim to the sun that it is not the ocean.

But we know this isn't true. The wave is never separate from the ocean just like our thoughts, no matter how inspired, can ever separate themselves from a consciousness we all share. No idea, no matter how original, can exist as something separate or unique from consciousness as a whole. Our bodies, our mental faculties, and creativity are just the messengers. We are the many hands and faces of a single being.

But we naturally don't see this. We don't see this because being everything and everyone as something infinite can seem frightful. It means you have nothing to hold on to. No name to wear, no identity to call home. You would have to reinvent yourself in every breath. Such a task!

And so in varying degrees, we instead settle for something less. We choose a name. We settle with a personality. Goals, values, a community — not so much out of choice, but out of pure coincidence. Out of pattern. And this newfound self we call home comes at the price of fragile expectations. Should any token of this lifestyle change, we fall to pieces.

And so we craft a talent out of ignoring things. We become a stranger to uncertainty and embrace a world of patterned and predictable life. A very real dilemma!

Yoga prescribes the antidote. To accept that you are everything. All things as one expression. You are the mountains. You are the breeze rattling the window. The bird among the rooftops. You are just as much your name and personality as you are the moon and passing clouds. And if anything ever happens to you, ask yourself — how does that effect the mountains? Has the breeze changed? Will the birds always sing?

Text 1.5

वृत्तयः पञ्चतय्यः क्लिष्टाक्लिष्टाः
vr̥ttayaḥ pañcatayyaḥ kliṣṭākliṣṭāḥ

vr̥ttayaḥ	Fluctuations, misconceptions
pañcatayyaḥ	Fivefold
kliṣṭa	Harmful, burdensome, afflicted
akliṣṭaḥ	Harmless, carefree, unafflicted

Our state of mind is broken into five affecting and non-affecting states.

Our state of mind isn't a force of nature. It is as simple as any garden. Anger, love, greed, fear — are all fruits of the same tree. If we learn the means of how this tree rows, how this consciousness develops, we can act without reacting. There will be no mystery to our passion.

This is how we break free from from the domino effect of coerced reaction. To understand consciousness, we must begin at the very root of all existence. Before sound. Before intention. Before anything at all. The late Ramana Maharshi offered a pathway to this origin by asking the question, who am I?

By asking this simple question, you'll eventually realize that who you are is what the world is. And what the world is, is what came before before us. Repeating this question like a mantra will lead you eventually all the way to the very beginning. To the fountainhead of existence. And it's from here, that when consciousness is born — it's born of into any combination of five affective and non-affective states.

Text 1.6

प्रमाण विपर्यय विकल्प निद्रा स्मृतयः
pramāṇa viparyaya vikalpa nidrā smṛtayaḥ

pramāṇa	Real knowledge, true perception
viparyaya	False knowledge, misconception
vikalpa	Imagination
nidrā	Deep unconscious sleep
smṛtayaḥ	Memory

The five types of thoughts are true, mistaken, imagined, unconsciousness, and remembered perception.

There are five kinds of thoughts. Each one born from varying layers of our awareness. From wherever they come, or whatever they are – they are the furthest after effect of a much deeper process from a much deeper awareness. Lets cycle through each of these five states of conscious development.

True perception, *pramāṇa,* is the equivalent of recognizing the moment you're in a dream. You are fully aware the context and setting is unreal including your awareness itself, but somehow you've realized you're dreaming. Your perception extends to a context greater than both the setting and the scope of seeing.

Mistaken perception, *viparyaya,* is the age-old adagé of seeing a snake in the road when it is actually only a stick. Our sense perception proves itself incapable of noticing the actual world around us. Instead what we see, is the coerced reaction based on scripted and patterned history we have experienced.

Imagination, *vikalpa,* is our sacred ability to conjur the world that isn't there. Unlike mistaken perception, *vikalpa* is an active process. One in which we are actively producing a mental description of things that do not exist.

Deep unconscious sleep, *nidrā,* is a very subtle but extremely powerful perception. The deeper we traverse into the realms of our unconsciousness, the deeper our awareness reflects the essence of our hereditary patterns, our species' patterns, and all the unconscious traits we acquired in our childhood. These themes always find a way into our waking life.

At every given moment, any given thought pattern, is unfolding in shades of each of these qualities all at the same time; true perception, false perception, imagination, the total void of perception, and memory. The goal behind classifying the growth of our consciousness into perception is so we can journey deeper into the subtle aspects of our awareness and the fruits of its labor.

Text 1.7

प्रत्यक्षानुमानाअगमाः प्रमाणानि

pratyakṣa-anumāna-āgamāḥ pramāṇāni

pratyakṣa	Sense perception
anumāna	Logic
āgamaḥ	Testimony, documentary knowledge
pramāṇāni	Real knowledge, true perception

The three interdependent ways to attain true knowledge is direct experience, a means to communicate with it, and an outside higher authority to justify it.

When is truth valid? Patanjali subscribes the aid of three suspects that are the cornerstone to validating what we believe to be true. We adopt them the way an engineer would adopt a bonafide floorplan to guarantee the structural integrity of a valuable architecture.

The first and most obvious is our direct experience. We see, touch, and smell all the attributes of this experience. We are convinced it is real. But our experience by itself may not necessarily make it real. We could be seeing a snake in the road when it is yet just another stick. We could be imagining ourselves enlightened when only our ego is having a spring break. Nevertheless, the process begins with our first contact and our personal conscious exchange.

We then employ logic. Logic works as a means of communication between a phenomena and an observer. Our main goal is to measure the distance between this object and what we consider to be ultimately truthful. How close to authenticity does this experience represent? Does it draw my own awareness to a more authentic and graceful place? Ideally, each question sobering up the experience to its reality.

But even our logic can be as flawed as our perception. The third milestone to perceiving truth is its testimony and authorization by someone or something else. Something outside of our own ego needs to also validate this truth.

Whether it is a holy text, a great sage, or the unscripted wilderness, we must not let our sole observation determine was it and is not. It is something we are entirely incapable of.

If all three of these gates can be crossed, then we can safely assume we are approaching truth. For example, to know the phenomena of love, we must first experience it. We must be able to communicate with it. And we must have it validated by some higher authority. Then we can know the love is true.

Experience without logic will leave us confused. Logic without experience or authority is superfluous. Authority without experience is corrupt. However, these three elements together work as a periscope on to the world.

Text 1.8

विपर्ययो मिथ्याज्ञानमतद्रूप प्रतिष्ठम्

viparyayo mithyā-jñānam-atadrūpa pratiṣṭham

viparyaya	False knowledge, error
mithyā	False
jñānam	Knowledge
atadrūpa	Not from nature, different
pratiṣṭham	Resting, established in

Unreal cognition develops from incorrect perception.

Very simply, you are what you eat. Consume your illusions, and you will become your illusions. See truth, and you are truth. But truth isn't something specific. It's not just the ecstacy of dance, or the sweet words of a teacher – it's also the anguish of hunger, and faceless drum of urban traffic. For the seeker, we must not insist that our truth is something good or bad. It is what it is. And for this reason, that soley focusing on things of good nature, or holy can also very easily be unreal, and cause us to become unreasonable people.

It's very common for us to use blinders in the spiritual path and very stubbornly refuse to accept a world outside of our beliefs. You could say it's helpful in some ways because we become more focused. However, in the long run, this supposed truth will depend on avoiding the authority of the real world. With no authority, we can not consider it a truth.

This happens in all sorts of ways. Sometimes we hold such a high standard of friendship that we sabotage our chances of having one. Sometimes we hold such a high standard of emotional reaction that we dare never to have one.

As the saying goes, there's no need to throw the baby out with the bath water. Both the path of our conscious awakening, and the distractions that destroy it are equally important. They must share the same space in our hearts. We may not be able to annihilate non-truth, but we can restfully understand where it's inertia leads, and why we shouldn't encourage it.

Text 1.9

शब्दज्ञानानुपाती वस्तुशून्यो विकल्पः
śabda-jñāna-anupātī vastu-śūnyo vikalpaḥ

śabda	Words
jñāna	Knowledge
anupātī	In sequence
vastu	Reality, an actual object
śūnya	Devoid of
vikalpaḥ	Imagination, illusion, conceptualization

Imagination is a word, sound, or expression where there is no such object or reality to it.

One of the first tools of humankind was our ability to share fiction. It came to us before the advent of the wheel, before fire, before even the spoken word. And it's the ability to share fiction that allows us to cooperate past the boundaries of natural law. Capitalism, religion, even human rights are all fictions that no natural law protects.

Remove any one of those fictions, and the forest will remain unphased. Simply because nature has no fiction. Animals, plants, and stones, the laws of physics do no cooperate with fiction. But we do.

And by sharing a common fiction, whether its money, or God, or the idea that all people are created equal, we can cooperate with each other beyond intercontinental borders. A feat no other living species on Earth has seemed to demonstrate.

But we forget so easily the relativity of this fiction. And all too easily we let the rules of our fiction destroy the same world that nature by itself could have resolved. Capitalism and God may have desecrated just as much life on Earth as it might have otherwise saved.

There is a very fine line that exists between this imagination and what is truth. And there is a tool for specifically balancing between reality and nonreality. It is called improvisation. Improvisation allows us to see two worlds simultaneously, by placing our awareness at the forefront of our fiction. Right as it's being written. And from this place, we can see how one side manifests the other. How the forest reflects the omnipotence of God, and how God reflects the omnipotence of the forest. How nature's will for need creates capitalism, and how capitalism reflects nature's will for survival.

Treat improvisation like a garden. Water it thoroughly with loving attention. Express yourself so feverishly that you can observe what's growing in this garden of yours. Are the fruits bitter and hurtful? Are they sweet and weightless? Who are you?

Text 1.10

अभावप्रत्ययाअलम्बना तमोवृत्तिर्निद्र

abhāva-pratyaya-ālambanā tamo-vr̥ttir-nidra

abhāva	Absence
pratyaya	Cause, instincts, intentions
ālambana	Support, based upon
tamo	Fluctuations, illusion
vr̥ttir	Thoughts, fluctuations
nidrā	Deep unconscious sleep

Dreamless sleep is the void of all thought patterns.

In a state of deep sleep, we no longer exist. Which is technically a very realistic state of consciousness. If it were possible to magically be aware of this experience, we would be looking from the ground up through the entire expansive architecture of our identity, our fears, and calculated personalities. But our feet would be firmly planted on a void. A place from which awareness resonates.

This is because at the depth of your consciousness, you are no one. A little higher, and you become your instincts, your fight or flight response, and biological need. A little bit higher, and your first efforts as an individual begin at your unconscious level where your dreams, your memories, and your history start crafting your responses for you. Eventually, you find the full faculties of your attention. It is from here that you can fully interact with the world consciously. But this state of mind is both a blessing and a curse.

In one sense, you are now a mirrored but fractured expression of pure awareness. You are the universe experiencing itself. But this experience is widely misunderstood. Once life realizes it is aware, it tends to believe that this awareness is somehow unique. It forgets that its own awareness is just a very humble link in a chain of awarenesses that lead to it. Struggle all you may to claim your individuality, but you are just a mirrored link among infinite others. And therefore, your so-called individuality is constantly in flux, reflecting the world around it. But these things are not you. Just as the rain isn't you when it lands on you.

You are still of the origin from which the unconscious rests upon; formless and eternal.

Text 1.11

अनुभूतविषयासंप्रमोषः स्मृतिः
anu-bhūta-viṣaya-asaṁpramoṣaḥ smr̥tiḥ

anu-bhūta	From that experience
viṣaya	Situation, object of senses
asaṁ	Incomplete
pramoṣaḥ	Elimination, shedding
smr̥tiḥ	Memory

Moments of experience that are not lost are called memory.

Our whole lives are mostly operated out of memory. Not just our memories, but our genetic memories. Memories that travel back in time generations. Memories inherited by species before us. Sometimes, a memory is so subtle, we're not even aware that we are remembering something. Memory also works as a duct-tape of conscious awareness. In the pot-holes of uncertainty that riddle the world around us, we patch it confidently with memory. Even if the memory is unreal.

Very easily the world around us can become a bricollage of things that never were. And since we're constantly patching what we don't know, the act of memorization becomes repetitive. But no truth is repetitive. Truth is a constant; always changing. Therefore, it should be impossible to remember. We can only memorize the steps that lead up to it, but not the notion of truth itself. Knowing how to both memorize, and not memorize will help us distinguish when a moment is a memory or a reality.

Text 1.12

अभ्यासवैराग्याअभ्यां तन्निरोधः
abhyāsa-vairāgya-ābhyāṁ tan-nirodhaḥ

abhyāsa	The career of practice
vairāgya	Nonattachment
ābhyāṁ	Both
tan	This
nirodha	To control, to let be

Practice and non-attachment is the process of mental mastery.

Our desires puppeteer us like a marionette. Rarely do we have a chance to act outside of these strings. Rarely do we have the ability to transcend our predefined reactions. Desires carve us out of stone. And as such, we become these rigid, stone-carved personalities. It is nearly impossible for us to recognize truth even if it were staring at us in the face.

Just as when Radhanath Swami met his spiritual master, Prabhupada. Radhanath eventually renounced his entire life, his career, and family to become a devotee of Prabhupada and renunciant for life. But when he first met him, he very naturally decided to continue searching elsewhere. It didn't hit right away. You could say, Radhanath's predefined responses still guided him. Just as our desires commandeer us regardless of what truth we may be fortunate to see.

It is the only obstacle to acknowledging truth. And the most powerful means to remove this obstacle is nonattachment or *vairāgya*. *Vairāgya* is a means of taking ownership of the body and mind. It is a career of abandoning the trivial in favor of the actual. And it begins by serving something greater than just our own desires.

We can transcend desire quite easily by simply finding something greater than just this body, or just our career, or whatever security we revolve around. Some of us accomplish this by serving their loved ones. The more pious among us reach out indiscriminately to anyone.

Others point to a God, a shared soul, or simply their will to love.

The goal is to elevate our taste to a more wholesome, inward life; a life fulfilled by its presence not its things. A goal to devote ourselves to something greater than just the self. This transforms the context of what we need. And a greater marionette takes over. A broader context ensues. And truth becomes available.

Text 1.13

तत्र स्थितौ यत्नोऽभ्यासः
tatra sthitau yatno-'bhyāsaḥ

tatra	Of these
sthitau	Continuously
yatna	Effort
abhyāsaḥ	Career of practice

One must be consistent in their practice by making the time to be present.

Our practice comes in two forms, the practice itself and our career of practicing. Both of them should be seen as separate yet interdependent skills we devote ourselves to. In order to meditate, you have to be just as devoted to the practice, as you do to affording the time to practice.

Being talented at yoga, or knowing by memory entire scriptures is meaningless if you have no time in your life to offer them as a daily practice. This is because consistency is paramount.

The subtle nuances of our awareness can only be uncovered by performing the same repetitive action day after day. By performing the same actions through the infinite masks we wear. The same actions through our victories and losses. It is only then can we see where the ego breaks, and truth emerges. It's only then can we see the difference between what serves our soul and what serves our inertia.

Each nuance acts as a trailhead to the immense uncharted territory of our heart and thought process. Like a lion among the grass, we wait and listen without hesitation, every morning, until the soul on its own volition comes to us. But if we are not consistent, if our practice is not regimented into our identity, then we will never crack the ego's puzzle. We can never transcend our desires if we only practice when we desire. We will, as Zen students are taught, be "a ghost clinging to the bushes and leaves." [Bassui]

Text 1.14

स तु दीर्घकाल नैरन्तर्य सत्काराअदराअसेवितो दृढभूमिः
sa tu dīrghakāla nairantarya satkāra-ādara-āsevito
dṛḍhabhūmiḥ

sa	The same [abhyāsaḥ]
tu	Furthermore
dīrgha	Long
kāla	Time
nairantarya	Uninterrupted
satkāra	True care, reverence
āsevito	Practiced
dṛḍha	Strong, firm
bhūmiḥ	Ground, Earth, basis

This practice, performed for a long time, without pause, and with sincere devotion will become the rock you stand on.

The ego is the glass ceiling to your physical, and emotional growth. Regardless of your determination or your feverish goals, so long as you are serving the ego, then the ego will always know how to excuse yourself from obtaining those goals.

This is why in yoga, we renounce the fruit of our labor. We do not act out of interest. We do so out of duty. Because this isn't about me, this is about truth. If we persist in this mindset, the context of our lives literally becomes the world we live within rather than the world we invent for ourselves. This subtle tweak of our perception goes very easily unnoticed.

For most of us, perception is the theatrics of our five senses, our state of mind, set and setting. But this is just the very beginning of it. Because behind the scaffolds of our awareness are thousands of mechanisms cut and carved by our desires, inertia, and will to survive. Mechanisms that can puppeteer and even coerce our senses into feeling, thinking, even seeing things that are not actually there. The practice, whatever it might be, is a hidden window in this sensory auditorium. If the practice is consistent, we can take a step outside, and see a world unscripted by our instincts and preprogrammed reactions. The practice itself becomes a transcendental sixth sense.

Once our practice leads us beyond the boundaries of our self-service, it becomes the platform from which we see. Much in the same way the body's senses serve the mind's perception. A consistent and uninterrupted practice serves as the eye for our truth's perception. And that becomes the rock we stand upon.

Text 1.15

दृष्टानुश्रविकविषयवितृष्णस्य वशीकारसंज्णा वैराग्यम्
dṛṣṭa-anuśravika-viṣaya-vitṛṣṇasya vaśīkāra-saṁjṇā vairāgyam

dṛṣṭa	The seen
ānuśravika	Heard of
viṣaya	Object of the senses
tṛṣṇa	Someone freed from craving
vaśikāra	Absolute control
saṁjñā	Consciousness
vairāgyam	Nonattachment

Mastery is attained when even things heard in scriptures are consciously let go of.

Words and logic are the furthest from the practice itself. It is only when we are severely separated from our hearts, can the first words appear. This is why religious extremists can argue uninterrupted for centuries. Or how academics can very easily dismiss the essence of a teaching. It is impossible to describe an essence with thought, words, or logic. Because their thirst for knowledge is coming from their ego instead of their heart, the only answer that will satisfy them is that which graces the same ego.

All religious traditions wax and wane with this frightful fungus of a commentary. Originally, Jesus was only his love and his miracles. Peter institutionalized them, and a church was born. A church which further inculcated a myriad of completely bizarre and unhelpful rules. Which culminated in Luther tearing down the walls of the institution and open sourcing once again the original love of Christ.

Zen Buddhism was born when Siddhartha held up a flower and without words, smiled at his disciple Ananda. Not before long, a religion was born, instititutionalized, and carried through India, China, and Japan. Books were written, laws were formed, and the nations adopted its beliefs as philosophical currency. That is until the illiterate water boy, Hui Neng, was given successorship of the tradition. He compassionately destroyed the institution, removed the laws, and ended the patriarchy.

In Hinduism, the Vedas colonialized the spoken word and traditions throughout India. Little by little, they separated the intention from the action, and ceremoniously decorated just the action. Not before long, there was very little intention and quite a lot of ceremony. It's then that by the 8th to 10th century, books such as the Yoga Sutras, and later Lord Caitanya's sankirtan movement sought to destroy the institution and return to the intention. To the heart of the practice.

In this verse, Patanjali is reminding us all humbly that there is greater value in our practice than there is in the texts that lead us there. Even this Yoga Sutras is incomparable to the heart you carry.

Text 1.16

तत्परं पुरुषख्यातेः गुणवैतृष्ण्यम्
tatparaṁ puruṣa-khyāteḥ guṇa-vaitr̥ṣṇyam

tat	That
paraṁ	Higher
puruṣa	Collective consciousness, true consciousness
khyāti	Experential knowledge
guṇa	The three qualities of nature [sattva, rajas, and tamas]
vaitr̥ṣṇyam	Indifference to craving

The purest consciousness is one that reflects indifference to the most subtle qualities.

Materialism is more addictive than any drug. We acquire it at such an early age, it's difficult to see how much it has affected our spirit. Especially if we live among fellow addicts. To see truth, to see the world outside of ourselves, we have to fight this craving. Until the craving is abated, our every decision, our every friend and foe we choose – will always be guided by material conquest. Just as to a drug addict, the drug comes first.

But even beneath this materialist landscape, there exists an even more subtle sense of reaction. Subtleties composed by our instincts, our will to survive, or the deep ocean of our subconscious. Reactions so subtle, they might appear as if they don't exist at all. But in the context of our entire lives, we can still observe a strain of their influence.

The goal of the awakened mind is equanimity even at this depth. Even among the elements the majority of us would consider impossible to traverse. An awareness tailored by the nurturing seeds of our practice until they grow into our nature. But how does one augment their consciousness to these depths? How can we alter our instincts when the human body, its hormonal and electrical messaging system is essentially faster than our awareness?

One small part of this answer is that all material originates in consciousness. The air between us, the floor we stand on, and the intricate network of bodily systems.

Everything begins and ends in awareness whether we as the individual are aware of it. The means in which to interact with this global awareness is by surrendering to pure uncertainty. By adopting improvisation, uncertainty, and compassion, we can delve into depths of awareness that do not allow a seeker, an object, or an action. And from this depth, we plant the seeds.

Text 1.17

वितर्कविचाराअनन्दास्मितारुपानुगमात्संप्रज्ञातः
vitarka-vicāra-ānanda-asmitā-rupa-anugamāt-
saṁprajñātaḥ

vitarka	Mundane thought, physical
vicāra	awareness
ānanda	Subtle thought
asmitā	Pure happiness
rūpa	Oneness of self and all
anugamāt	Form, nature
saṁprajñāta	Resulting in
	Absolute knowledge

Absolute knowledge is composed of four layers; thought and reasoning, the emotional response, causeless bliss, and oneness.

Anyone can witness a lightbulb pop and shatter. But knowing where the lightbulb was and why it happened is called context. Context is enlightenment. True knowledge is knowing the greatest of all contexts. You could say the entirety of our spiritual practice is the humble and endless effort to broaden this context. To see life in all its majesty in its most honest way, from the eyes of all of its inhabitants; both living and nonliving.

We approach this context just, like any relationship, in layers. When we first approach the idea of enlightenment, the relationship begins with lots of ideas, thoughts, books, and quotes. Perhaps we attend lectures or retreats. The reason is because the furthest thing from our truth is words and logic. It acts as the pawn and the very front gate of our true selves. Whenever we meet someone new, before we let them into our lives, we begin by examining their social acumen.

Should they pass our tests and appeal to our sentiments, we let them in. The philosophy of enlightenment begins to brush against our hearts. We begin to feel something rather than think something. Just as a stranger can become promoted to a friend. They're less a logical aspect of our intellect, and more like the furniture in our hearts. But our emotional wellbeing has its own gauntlet of bureaucracy. Our heart also has many tests that an entity must traverse in order to go deeper.

If the heart is consistently comforted, if our emotional wellbeing was never betrayed, this foreign entity travels deeper. Past the third gate into a confidential place within our awareness where we experience absolute indiscriminate bliss. It's technically a place we always have access to. Our absolute happiness is always there. But for the materialist addict, our happiness has to be earned by materialism. It has to be justified. There has to be materialist reason. And so at this point, the knowledge has proven itself to us logically and emotionally. We are comforted. So we open our gates to experience incalculable bliss from it.

At this point, if this pure bliss continues uninterrupted, the knowledge travels to the deepest aspect of the consciousness. A doorway that when crossed, destroys the perceiver completely. They become one. They discover that they were never separate. And that the knowledge was since the very beginning only reflecting their nature.

Text 1.18

विरामप्रत्ययाभ्यासपूर्वः संस्कारशेषोऽन्यः
virāma-pratyaya-abhyāsa-pūrvaḥ saṁskāra-śeṣo-'nyaḥ

virāma	To end, to let go
pratyaya	Perception, impression
abhyāsa	The career of practice
pūrvaḥ	Previous
saṁskāra	Unconscious impressions,
śeṣa	instincts
anyaḥ	Remainder
	The other

In this sutra, we describe objectless samadhi. Where cessation of our cognition as a practice will lead us beyond the residual cognitive imprints.

Effortless effort, causeless cause, see without seeing, are all using our vernacular to describe something outside of a vernacular's ability. No language will be able to describe how we really feel, let alone what rests below the surface of our emotions.

As we are taught in the Zen tradition, if you see the Buddha in the road, kill him. Because our logic nor our assumptions can deliver the entire way to the source. Eventually, we will have to abandon the holy books, our teachers, our shoes, and eventually our souls.

Our spiritual materialism can harm us as much as it helps us. Even the pearl of our holy aspirations may also be lying to us. So the non-objectivist obeys no-thought. She or he will surrender their ego to pure uncertainty as means to perceive the world without discrimination; an entryway to honesty.

This sutra does not negate the previous sutra on objectful samadhi. In fact, in its own rebellious way, it's offering two ways to the same goal. Both worshiping a locus, and serving nondualism. A higher practitioner will eventually be unable to distinguish one from the other even though they are described as entirely opposite.

Text 1.19

भवप्रत्ययो विदेहप्रकृतिलयानम्
bhava-pratyayo videha-prakr̥ti-layānam

bhava	Developing, birth
pratyayaḥ	Perception, impression
videha	Beings without bodies
prakr̥ti	Matter
laya	Merged
prakr̥ti-layānam	Those merged in matter

There are some beings without bodies or who are only slightly merged in the material world.

Every movement, every growth in the world begins with pure consciousness. That consciousness forms intentions and those intentions form into movement, and movement into beings. The history of our biological evolution is essentially a series of these conscious driven intentions. Then out of every life, that original pure consciousness continues to echo into our cultures, our spoken tongue, and our faculty of sense. The whole enterprise begins with the subtle origin of formless pure consciousness.

This sutra describes a very subtle place just a fraction of a distance between pure consciousness and the material world. It describes a living being who only exist in pure consciousness. They have no actual bodies, and they are only slightly still affiliated with the material world. Think of them as bodies of intention.

They move like the weather, inhabiting the culture, thoughts, and creative movement of receptive peoples and creatures. An intention by itself can not live without a body to perform its effort. And so they travel from the subtle realms of pure consciousness and puppeteer the world around us.

When we can see this world of influence, and see the forces that work outside the boundaries of human authority, we then see how inept the human senses are at truly experiencing pure consciousness. The body in and of its self is already so far away.

Text 1.20

श्रद्धावीर्यस्मृति समाधिप्रज्ञापूर्वक इतरेषाम्

śraddhā-vīrya-smr̥ti samādhi-prajñā-pūrvaka itareṣām

śraddhā	Faith
vīrya	Vigor, determination
smr̥ti	Memory
prajñā	Wisdom
samādhi	Pure equal consciousness, a state of mind
pūrvaka	Preceded by
itareṣā	For others

The path is made of faith, conviction, awareness, absorption, and wisdom.

The practice is a long and beaten path. It's treds are carved by countless souls who came before you. If we are humble enough, we can follow in the footsteps of giants. If we are perilous, we can carve our own. Whichever way we go, the path is written by five values.

The first is faith because everything begins with the belief that this will solve something. Perhaps we see someone far uphead – lighter, effulgent, and at peace. Or perhaps we noticed a flower breaking through a concrete sidewalk, erupting toward the sun. A feat, one would wonder, is possible for maybe us.

This experience hardens within us and turns into conviction. We acquire a higher taste for life. One equal to our faith. We observe everyday, every choice, every experience from the perspective of that lighter, effulgent, and peaceful person. From the perspective of that rebel flower. Where faith is the spark, conviction is the fire.

What sustains that fire is memory. This path should be seen like a lover. One in which we're constantly thinking of it, constantly seeking their approval, constantly conjuring up creative ways to please them. An urge of longing that sneaks into us from a deep and transcendental place.

It comes from our soul's feverish will to connect with what was lost. And what was lost was our knowledge that we are at rest and entirely fulfilled. That we are, and always will be the love that we seek. And anything we can do to remind ourselves of this, whether it is in every breath, or in every waking step, we can keep ourselves securely on the path.

And then one day the path becomes us. In a matrimony of total absorption, we lose the self, and become the path. Our breath, our thoughts, our friends and projects – everything is inseperable from the practice itself. There is no longer one who walks upon the path, nor is there something to walk upon. We become the entire expression of both the path and the being.

And then there finally is wisdom. From this selfless home, words and actions will echo back into the hands that brought them there. We speak on behalf of the path.

Text 1.21

तीव्रसंवेगानामासन्नः
tīvra-saṁvegānām-āsannaḥ

tīvra	Speedy, keen
saṁvegāna	Equal intensity
āsannaḥ	Nearness

Our progress is determined by the rate at which we practice and the enthusiasm of that practice.

The goal of yoga is to find our origin. It's a very long distance goal, and to achieve this goal, we must be equipped to steer our lives through many obstacles over the course of many decades. Perhaps, lifetimes. No matter what the goal is, the two best methods for attaining it are consistency and joy.

Better than practicing for three hours just once a month is practicing daily for five minutes. Consistency is paramount to familiarlizing ourselves with the subtle details of our truth. No one's going to perfect the nuances of a particular Bach piece by crash-studying it once or twice a month. Even if you were gifted in music, the true apprehension of studying a musical composition doesn't come when you have learned the notes. It comes when you have embodied the piece. When you are fully enveloped in its movement, and to the listener, one would not be able to differentiate between the music and the musician.

Embodiment does not arrive simply out of consistency alone. There must be a burning willingness in our practice that drives us there. An insatiable loving devotion should be the vehicle our consistency is delivered on. A will to practice without any interest in receiving anything in return. To practice for the sake of practice. As a tree grows simply because it is a tree.

The complete embodiment of our practice, our truest presence, is not something we can demand. It is awarded only to patience. For those who know how to surrender their anxiety, prestige, and identity. Presence is only awarded to those who allow themselves to lose themselves to something outside of themselves. It may require an eternity, but we will get there by consistency and enthusiasm.

Text 1.22

मृदुमध्याधिमात्रत्वात्ततोऽपि विशेषः
mr̥du-madhya-adhimātratvāt-tato'pi viśeṣaḥ

mr̥dum	Mild
madhya	Moderate
adhimātravāt	Because of intensity
tataḥ	From this [this practice]
api	Also
viśeṣaḥ	Distinction

This practice comes in varying degrees of immersion; mild, moderate, and intense.

This sutra and the previous describe the architecture of presence. In 1.21, we learn frequency and conviction. In 1.22, we learn varying degrees of immersion. There's an ebb and flow between frequency, consistency, and immersion. Your conviction is what brings you to presence. Immersion is the level in which you surrender to it.

You can observe this surrendering in the way a violinist surrenders to their music, or a dancer disappears into a melody. Their conviction leads them to a cliff edge for them to leap from, and they leap into a presence as uncertain as it is graceful.

When I wake up at 5AM to practice, it's very common for me to begin my day with, "Why not just drink tea and browse the internet today instead," and when I start practicing, "let's just do a little practice today," or "let's skip the difficult parts" – this kind of chatter will go on until the moment I give up, give in, and become my breath.

Suddenly, there's no longer a commentator, and in the most materialistic sense, everything is so much easier. I lose myself to the practice. No longer is there someone practicing. It's just the practice itself happening. Now that the space is clear, a meditation may occur.

The depth in which we surrender to our art is always equal to the ease and brilliance in which the craft becomes.

Text 1.23

ईश्वरप्रणिधानाद्वा
īśvara-praṇidhānād-vā

īśvara	God, the form of God
pranidhāna	consciousness
vā	Absolute devotion
	Or

Devotion and surrendering to our source will lead to samadhi.

Like Sisyphus, our fated Greek hero, who for an eternity must roll the heaviest of rocks to the top of a mountain. Only to be to surprised that when he reaches the top, the rock slips and falls back to the bottom of the mountain. He then must return to the bottom, and attempt the long and arduous journey again and again.

He is not aware of himself performing this same action over and over, lifetime after lifetime. He is lead by an illusive materialism that the achievement of placing the rock on top of the mountain will somehow satisfy him. But Sisyphus will never find this satisfaction. Just like anyone of us will never find any sort of satisfaction from a material world. For every achievement we acquire, we lose another. And again, we scramble to the bottom of the mountain to struggle our ways up again. This time we think it will be different. But I assure you it never will. Patanjali in this sutra, offers the cure.

The cure to Sisyphus' dilemma is finding unconditional love for his rock. Sisyphus could for just a moment expand the context of his goals to something greater than just his rock and greater than getting it to the top of the hill. If Sisyphus sees the act of merely pushing the rock as the most beautiful and selfless way to serve the Lord, then he will feel complete immediately regardless of whether the rock has reached the top or if it has fallen again. When we offer our pain and our struggle as a gift of unconditional love, as a service -- then that love will pierce through whatever unimaginable struggle we live among. Because it's no longer about us. It's no longer about the rock, or wherever we made it to, or however weak and tired we become. It's just about having the opportunity to serve. Which is always available.

A love so pure, that even if Sisyphus was offered relief from his work, he would refuse such an offer just to continue laboring for that eternal and uninterrupted warmth that is the love of *īśvara-praṇidhānād* or whatever is your penultimate source of devotion.

Text 1.24

क्लेश कर्म विपाकाअशयैःअपरामृष्टः पुरुषविशेष ईश्वरः
kleśa karma vipāka-āśayaiḥ-aparāmṛṣṭaḥ puruṣa-viśeṣa īśvaraḥ

kleśa	Obstacles
karma	Cause and effect, the physics
vipāka	of motion
āśayaiḥ	Fruition of actions
aparāmṛṣṭaḥ	The residue of our actions
puruṣa	Unaffected
viśeṣa	The unchanging, original
īśvaraḥ	seer
	Special
	God, the form of God
	consciousness

Causes, reactions, pain, or actions, do not effect the consciousness of God.

Awareness begins as an untouchable and eternal origin. Whatever it touches, it brings to life. We only experience a fraction of this awareness through taste, touch, and sensory theater. But just like that awareness, we can use that fractured form of it and bring to life inanimate objects. Our awareness can make a puppet or a computer come to life. The puppet nor the computer is conscious, but our awareness magically transforms these otherwise inanimate objects to life. And they suddenly reflect our fractured awareness.

The mind is not very different. It is also an inanimate tool used as an extension of something greater. Just as a puppet or any ordinary computer is an extension of consciousness, our mind is an extension of a greater awareness. And as a result, we come to life. We become animated. Just as the puppet reflects the puppeteer, we reflect whomsoever this greater awareness is.

And we can actually tiptoe backwards towards this original consciousness. By unraveling every obfuscating layer, we can peak into this conscious source. We start with the body, and its incredible design of tension. Billions of years of tension and release that have designed every organ, bone, and blood vessel. Every muscular apparatus, every movement, all designed by some sort of evolutionary ebb and flow.

Beneath this layer, we find an ornate masterpiece of emotion. Feelings composed of sensory theater, abstract thought, and phenomenal memories. It's a magnum opus of thought written and inherited through wombs of countless beings.

Beneath emotion, we find our will to survive.

Beneath survival, we find coincidence.

And at the very bottom, at the very beginning, we find original awareness. A pure and limitless consciousness. A creative source that manifests the awareness that animates us, and through us, everything we touch. It flows from an origin that can not be touched. It exists before reason and logic. Before time and space. Even the universe is its shadow.

Text 1.25

तत्र निरतिशयं सर्वज्ञबीजम्
1.25 tatra niratiśayaṁ sarvajña-bījam

tatra	There in [God]
sarvajña	All knowledge
niratiśayam	Unsurpassed
bījam	Seed, an origin

In God consciousness, there is a seed of all unsurpassed knowledge.

Selfless devotion is the most accurate platform to build knowledge from. Instead of learning what serves us, we learn by serving. It's two completely different knowledges. One of which is severely handicapped.

For example, if the platform was power and wealth, then the knowledge could mean knowing market manipulation, human resourcing, and real estate. If the platform was survival, then the knowledge is an acumen in fear and comfort. These are indeed knowledges. They have been developed and handed down through generations of academia. But they are all limited by our finite desires. They all can only grow as much as what serves us.

But if the platform is love, then the knowledge has no boundaries. Because from this platform, whatever we study, can exist outside the boundaries of what serves us. And since what serves us is dwarfed by what doesn't, we can access a broader knowledge. A kind of knowing that is more than just recalling a specific place in time, or the name of some forgotten word. Instead, it's knowing the perfect presence. And with it, manifesting a world to learn from.

Text 1.26

स एष पूर्वेषामपिगुरुः कालेनानवच्छेदात्

sa eṣa pūrveṣām-api-guruḥ kālena-anavacchedāt

pūrveṣām	Of the ancients
api	Also
guruḥ	Teacher, master
kāla	Time
anavacchedāt	Not being limited

In the very beginning, there were also teachers since truth is not limited by time.

The greatest knowledge is not passed by words. It's passed by association. Whether it is an association with nature or an association with a teacher. This teacher may come in all shapes and forms, and has existed since the beginning of time. This is why all beings, plants, animals, and insects should be seen as capable of being both your greatest teacher and your most feverish student. This is why chanting of the word *aum* is seen as both a teaching and echo that originated from the inception of the universe to its next.

And so, out of respect to this dialogue of truth, we listen to all.

Text 1.27

तस्य वाचकः प्रणवः
tasya vācakaḥ praṇavaḥ

tasya	Who posesses [God]
vācakaḥ	Designation, indicator, term
praṇavaḥ	The mystical syllable Aum literally translates to "humming"

We refer to this entire experience as Aum.

God has many names. Each one is a cognitive bookmark in our thoughts to refer to something all encompassing. Another name for God is simply context. The greater the context, the greater our sense of awareness. By thinking or speaking this referential name, the context of our immediate perception reflects how great of a context this God means to us. So simply by uttering one simple word, we can elevate our state of mind to reference all things all at once. Not just one temporary material thing like our hunger or our passions.

Whether we're aware of it or not, we're always chanting something. And whatever we chant, that is we we are. That is what we become. Most of the time, we are not aware of this chanting. Sometimes we chant, "money, money, money", or "power, power, power", or "self image, me, I am", and the context of our lives reflects it. We become our own island. Our world becomes smaller. We become more superficial. We can't both want power and self-image and have room for other people. The world won't be able to share a life with us. But if you're interested in sharing the world, then you must broaden the context of your life to encompass all of life.

And Patanjali suggests that we accomplish that by using a word as a spiritual bookmark. A word that can reference wherever we last left off in the progress of our conscious awakening. A word, that by itself, can refer not just the context of our consciousness, but the origin of all creation. And we can do this by lovingly referring to God, or Aum, or the sound of all.

The reason *praṇavaḥ*, which translates to humming, is used to describe the word, God – is, we believe, a humming like *aum* can be heard in all sound. The word *aum* is capable of referencing all sound just as it is intended to reference the source of all creation. From the trees swaying in an Autumn breeze, the cry of the morning rooster, the insects, and our voices. Everything, whether they are aware of it or not, is crying out to *īśvaraḥ*. They are, just as a flower imitates the sun, expressing their origin.

Text 1.28

तज्जपः तदर्थभावनम्
taj-japaḥ tad-artha-bhāvanam

taj-japaḥ	Whose repetition
tad	It [Aum]
artha	Meaning
bhāvanam	Dwelling upon, developing

Repetitive chanting of this Name will develop its meaning.

Its very natural for chanting to feel meaningless the first times we practice. Whether the word is Krishna, God, Jesus, Allah, or simply Aum it is only a word at face value. But each time the word is used, it will capture the state of mind you held while you last said it.

It can work adversely as well. Some people stub their toe and scream "G—d—mit!". It's no wonder that those same people usually share a disinterest in the concept of God. They've bookmarked the name of God as something only useful for blaming their pain on something or someone else.

But when we compose ourselves to chant with love and admiration, then that love and admiration becomes bookmarked in the word that led us there. So that at every time we repeat the word, we return to that same state of mind, and further the spiritual bookmark in our hearts. Each time, a little further. As Prabhupada said, no matter how far you veer from the spiritual path, once you return, you pick up right where you left off.

Text 1.29

ततः प्रत्यक्चेतनाधिगमोऽप्यन्तरायाभवश्च

tataḥ pratyak-cetana-adhigamo-'py-antarāya-abhavaś-ca

tataḥ	From this
pratyak	Inner
cetanā	Consciousness, the seer
adhigamo	Realization
api	Also
antarāyaḥ	Obstacles
abhāvaḥ	Absence
ca	And

From the loving repetition of the Name, comes the remover of all obstacles.

Touching the idea of universal love, or universal consciousness, or simply God, can paint a single stroke with a single breath. You won't see it at first, but over the course of several months, then several years, then several lifetimes, those millions of collected strokes will form a painting. A painting that can be so poignant, that others won't have to work as hard as you did to realize the same *samadhi.*

This painting is a world where instead of chasing after the ghosts and loose leaves that come and go, we teach ourselves to love without reason. This is why there are no obstacles to the yogi. Because there is no goals. There is no ends. There is only the means; the will to love found in every breath.

Text 1.30

व्याधि स्त्यान संशय प्रमादाअलस्याविरति
भ्रान्तिदर्शनालब्धभूमिकत्वानवस्थितत्वानि चित्तविक्षेपाः ते अन्तरायाः
vyādhi styāna saṁśaya pramāda-ālasya-avirati
bhrāntidarśana-alabdha-bhūmikatva-anavasthitatvāni
citta-vikṣepāḥ te antarāyāḥ

vyādhi	Disease
styāna	Apathy
saṁśaya	Doubt
pramāda	Neglect
ālasya	Sloth
avirati	Desire
bhrāntidarśana	Blind opinion
alabdha-bhūmikatva	Not obtaining ground
anavasthitatvāni	Instability, inconsistency
citta	Mind, thought
vikṣepaḥ	Distractions, lack of clarity
te	These
antarāyaḥ	Obstacles

There are a variety of distractions that will lead to a variety of disruptions.

To understand distraction, we need to first ensure that our mind has single-pointed focus. When our attention is single-pointed, then our distractions have context. If we are not focused, then our Truth is just as ambiguous as our distractions.

You might be doing something terrible with your life, and notice a butterfly outside and the feeling of running into the wild. But then you think this is a distraction, where in fact, it is your Path asking you to return.

Likewise, you might be steadfast in a yoga asana, sweating, a sudden wave of fear climbs over you, and you find yourself weeping. Your fear is asking you to run away, but this is a distraction that is taking you away from the Path.

Distractions might come in many forms, some helpful and some not. But we can know the difference by training the mind to have a single-pointed focus. In this way, the distractions, helpful or otherwise, become secondary to the practice itself.

Text 1.31

दुःखदौर्मनस्याङ्गमेजयत्वश्वासप्रश्वासाः विक्षेप सहभुवः
duḥkha-daurmanasya-aṅgamejayatva-śvāsapraśvāsāḥ
vikṣepa sahabhuvaḥ

duḥkha	Pain, suffering
daurmanasya	Frustration, melancholy
aṅgamejayatva	Trembling of the limbs
śvāsa-praśvāsaḥ	Inhaling, exhaling
vikṣepa	Distraction
sahabhuvaḥ	Symptoms, occur with

Pain, frustration, restlessness, irregularities of the breath are all symptoms of distractions.

Pain is the first and most common distraction. Pain can happen effortlessly. You can lock your keys out of the car, stub your toe, and pay your taxes and immediately move on. The pain was there, but now it isn't. The reason pain doesn't just magically vanish is because we covet the experience. We felt dishonered so we hold on to it as evidence. We explore where the entry wound was and compose a commentary. Nonsense! It's over, and now you're distracted from your presence.

Try rationalizing your pain with your breath instead of your thoughts. Instead of a commentary and an important looking briefcase to keep your suffering in, try something different. Offer a space for your pain to exist, to pass, and be forgotten. The cure is patience. Even these things too shall pass.

Frustration, fidgeting, an uneven breath; these are all habits of someone without patience. Patience is not someone who can wait. It's someone who can allow. Someone who can just accept whatever the world is whenever it is. And never be distracted from their presence.

Your breath can be the beauty of that presence. The consistency of that breath is your canary in the mines of conscious awareness.

Text 1.32

तत्प्रतिषेधार्थमेकतत्त्वाभ्यासः
tat-pratiṣedha-artham-eka-tattva-abhyāsaḥ

tat	These [distractions]
pratiṣedh	Diminish, fade
artam	For the sake of
eka	One
tattva	Truth
abhyāsaḥ	The career of practice

In order to overcome these obstacles, practicing a single truth is the way.

Single-pointed concentration is a sacred balance between focus and *vairagya,* non-attachment. The reason we run in place in our dreams is because we only have focus and no *vairagya*. And sometimes, we're lost from this world because we have so much *vairagya* and no focus.

But in the sacred middle, we can observe the world without touching it. Like watching a spinning globe of the Earth that will continue to spin if only we don't poke our commentary into what we think the world is. The moment we label it, and decorate it with emotion, we lose its grace. We lose the spin.

So instead, let the world go. We broaden the context beyond our own pain, beyond the world's pain, to the essence that is the origin of all consciousness. There are no obstacles when the heart is in that state. And there is no distance in knowing that heart.

Text 1.33

मैत्री करुणा मुदितोपेक्षाणांसुखदुःख पुण्यापुण्यविषयाणां भावनातः
चित्तप्रसादनम्

maitrī karuṇā mudito-pekṣāṇāṁ-sukha-duḥkha puṇya-apuṇya-viṣayāṇāṁ bhāvanātaḥ citta-prasādanam

maitrī	Friendliness
karuṇā	Empathy, compassion
mudito	Joy
upekṣana	Equanimity, indifference
sukha	Happiness, enjoyment
duḥkha	Suffering, pain
puṇya	Virtue
apuṇya	Vice
viṣayānam	Situations, occurences
bhāvanātaḥ	Developing
citta	Mind, that which is changeable
prasādanam	Lucity, rendering clear

When others are at bliss, be blissful. When they are not, be compassionate. When they are virtuous, be encouraging. When they are not, be indifferent.

What ties together all of these reactions is non-attachment, *vairagya*. Let people be themselves. You can't change them because they are working through generations of karma handed down to them. The very least we can do, is acknowledge their current state of mind. Acknowledge the cause of their context, and let go of our own.

To help unravel this experience, lets examine how we usually react to others. When we are not dwelling inwards, we are seeking our identity outwards. Constantly foraging our identity, wellbeing, and inspiration in the phenomenon of our senses. We endanger ourselves when we allow everything that we are to mirror anything that happens to be. Our identity begins to naturally prey on a diet of constant outward stimulus.

Without being aware of its cause, we slowly become increasingly defensive against what makes us calm, what makes us angry, what helps us sleep, what gives us a sense of belonging. Our fight or flight response becomes fully engaged. And people are the strongest emotional influence in this karmic identity.

Association may still be the greatest meditation. Where our community is a reflection of our subtle consciousness, we can carefully choose our associations to design our state of mind. But it is also important to guard against our identity being continuously fueled and funded by a totally, abstract, and extremely unstable phenomenon of experience. Who ultimately defines what is a good culture versus "bad culture" is limited by their gross senses.

There's a careful balance. And the answer is to simply let them be while guarding your commitment to remain unattached and compassionate.

Text 1.34

प्रच्छर्दनविधारणाअभ्यां वा प्राणस्य
pracchardana-vidhāraṇa-ābhyāṁ vā prāṇasya

pracchardana	By exhaling
vidhāraṇa	Withholding
ābhya	Both
vā	Or
prāṇasya	Breath or energy

One approach is the gentle exhalation and regulation of the breath.

The breath is the cornerstone to life and realization. So long as we assume this body, we have the breath at our disposal. This is why, cognitively, it is a paramount instrument to incorporate in a practice that should be as available to us as air. We can use the breath as an anchor to our path, teaching ourselves that to breathe, means to be here, to be one, to be love.

In this way, wherever we are, whom ever we become, our breath will by itself direct us back to our practice. The breath is unique because unlike the heartbeat, it can be as expressive and flexible as a dancer. In this way, not only can you use the breath to remind yourself to return, but further, you can train yourself to be the improvisational and impulsive expression that is your heart. Own the breath, and you will share the world.

Text 1.35

विषयवती वा प्रवृत्तिरुत्पन्ना मनसः स्थिति निबन्धिनी
viṣayavatī vā pravr̥tti-rutpannā manasaḥ sthiti nibandhinī

viṣayavatī	Sensations
vāt	Or
pravrtti	Thought patterns, inclination towards thought
utpannā	Arising
manasaḥ	Of the mind
sthiti nibandhanī	Pulling together steadiness

Another practice to steady the mind is becoming hyper-aware of the senses.

The world can make it hard to feel. So we exaggerate what feeling we have left with things like caffeine, drugs, or television. But these things perpetuate the cycle, the lack of feeling, the need to continue taking more stimulants. But if all gross stimulants were removed, and we've taken the time to reacquaint ourselves in a world without loud, attention-grabbing stimuli, we begin to have an entirely different experience. In fact, we eventually don't need a stimulant at all.

We can stimulate sense by just acknolwedging sense. For example, taste. Instead of altering the quality of what you taste, just give yourself space to taste. Take three breaths patiently before you eat. Suddenly, the food will taste sweeter. Take three breaths before you turn on your favorite music, and the music will sound better. Take three breaths before you call your friend, and you'll have a more meaningful conversation.

In each of these examples, by simply embodying the senses, we become aware of apparatus we operate from; our consciousness. It allows us to question why the quality of our experience depends on space between our senses and our experience. This medium of thought will lead you to the deeper parts of Chapter 3 and 4 in the Yoga Sutras where Patanjali illustrates where these practices eventually lead.

Text 1.36

विशोका वा ज्योतिष्मती
viśokā vā jyotiṣmatī

viśokā	Painless
vāt	Or
jyotiṣmatī	Effulgent inner light

Another practice is dwelling in a state of light, free of pain.

This is another example of objective meditation. When you focus on any creative expression such as peace or any name of God or simply love. We are attempting to immerse ourselves until a point of absolute disillusionment and origin. You can think of each these objective meditations as a separate trailhead to the same peak.

Patanjali calls this *jyotiṣmatī*, an effulgent, painless inner light. To focus on an origin that floods the world with life through painless light. By painless, we infer that there is no sufferer nor suffering because that being comes before a world of pleasure and pain. A place that is the genesis of experience. Where the shadow of duality has yet to occur. It is a fountainhead. The closer we are to that fountainhead, the least we are concerned with the workings and matter of a material world.

In short, be light.

Text 1.37

वीतराग विषयम् वा चित्तम्
vītarāga viṣayam vā cittam

vīta	To be without
raga	Desire
viṣayam	Objects of the senses
vā	Or
cittam	Though patterns, that which is changeable

Another practice, is to practice having no desires or no object of the senses.

This is called non-objective meditation. When there is no object of focus. No God, no light and dark, or opinion. Our focus is very simply awareness. Pure awareness. An awareness that we have reason to believe exists well before we do. And who we are, our emotionally riddled senses, are only an obfuscation of this original awareness.

Just as a violinst and their violin become indistinguishable in the grace of their music, the seeker who seeks awareness and pure awareness also become indistinguishable. They become another small example of the universe experiencing itself through itself.

This experience has an enormous impact on our *karmasya*, our storehouse of karma. As we essentially are what we experience, and when we experience something that transends the senses, our identity becomes an extension of pure awareness not our superfluous interests and disinterests.

Who exactly is that person? When there is no longer an impetus of interest, eventually there is no observer to notice. The world around you becomes the living being, and the seeker is its atom. Our actions as an individual become indistinguishable from a falling leaf, not by an opinion.

Text 1.38

स्वप्ननिद्रा ज्ञानाअलम्बनम् वा
svapna-nidrā jñāna-ālambanam vā

svapna	Dream
nidrā	Deep unconscious sleep
jñāna	Knowledge
ālambana	Based upon, supported by
vā	Or, also

Another practice is learning lucid dreaming.

Dreams and waking life is not so black and white. Where does a dream begin and end? Perception is always a gradient of lucidity against a gradient of imagination whether you call it a dream or not. The borders of perception are both ephemeral and hallucinagenically dynamic.

There is, in every manner, times when we are dreaming while awake, or asleep yet entirely aware. Just as there are times when we render only some of our waking life with reality, and the rest with imagination. As the Vedantic metaphor goes, when the stick lays in the road, it can also be the memory of a snake.

Becoming aware of these borders, and recognizing you are dreaming is called lucid dreaming. This ability is not just limited to becoming aware of a dream from inside of a dream. But more so, becoming aware of our experience as a whole whether it's a dream or not. Becoming aware of the borders of our exhaustion, our senses, our living experience, and being capable of observing this phantasmagoria outside the scope of being awake or dreaming. An elevated state that transcends the world of imagination and reality.

Eventually the seeker will realize that the dream had always been indistinguishable from whatever we affectionally described as a waking state.

Text 1.39

यथाअभिमतध्यानाद्वा
yathā-abhimata-dhyānād-vā

yatha	According to
ābhimata	That which is attractive
dhyānād	Meditation
vā	Or

At last, just meditate according to whatever you choose.

Single-pointed focus is the goal. The object is whatever illustrates you. Watching television, listening to music may gather your attention for a moment, but only within the context of the TV show, or that particular song.

The object's value to your meditation is relative to how encompassing it is to life as a whole. The breath is greater than a candlelight. The ocean is greater than the rain. The goal is to constantly seek a broader context to focus on, whatever it may be called in this lifetime, and serve it.

Text 1.40

परमाणु परममहत्त्वान्तोऽस्य वशीकारः
paramāṇu parama-mahattva-anto-'sya vaśīkāraḥ

parama	Smallest, greatest
aṇu	Atom, preceded by
parama	Smallest, greatest
mahattva	Great truth
antah	Up to
asya	The yogi's
vaśīkāraḥ	Mastery

Whatever practice you have chosen, the mind will master the ability to focus on the smallest to the largest points of focus.

Mastering the mind is the very first step. Just like when the dancer's body is mastered in strength and flexibility, beauty follows. When the surfer learns the macro and micro balances of their weight against an uncertain and changing world, what's left to be seen, is their soul dancing among uncertain waves. When the mind has mastered the context of perception, the lotus unfolds.

Text 1.41

क्षीणवृत्तेरभिजातस्येव मणेर्ग्रहीतृग्रहणग्राह्येषु तत्स्थतदञ्जनता समापत्तिः

kṣīṇa-vṛtter-abhijātasy-eva maṇer-grahītṛ-grahaṇa-grāhyeṣu tatstha-tadañjanatā samāpattiḥ

kṣīna	Weakened, reduced
vṛttiḥ	Thought patterns
abhijātasya	Of high quality [
eva	transparent]
maṇi	Like
grahītṛ	Diamond, jewel
grahaṇa	The knower
grāhyeṣu	The knowing
tatstha	The known
tadañjanatā	That which is situated
samāpattiḥ	Taking the form of one another
	Total absorption [samadhi]

When our superfluous thoughts are diminished, the mind becomes its true nature, transparent like a crystal, and thus can take on the qualities and completely absorb the object of your attention.

For most people, we rarely see the world outside of our own fantasy. But when the inertia of our illusion fades, we can start observing the world outside of ourselves. And when you notice the world outside of yourself, you realize there was never a difference between this so called world and this so called self.

We are, as Patanjali describes, a crystal reflecting the color around us. *Samapattih* means complete absorption. Meaning, for the enlightened mind, the world can be seen through you, and you among the world.

Text 1.42

तत्र शब्दार्थज्ञानविकल्पैः संकीर्णा सवितर्का समापत्तिः
tatra śabdārtha-jñāna-vikalpaiḥ saṁkīrṇā savitarkā samāpattiḥ

tatra	There
śabda	Word
artha	Meaning
jñāna	Knowledge
vikalpaḥ	Imagination, illusion
saṁkīrṇa	Mixed with
savitarka	Acknowledging
samāpattiḥ	Total absorption [samadhi]

The first of four layers to understand *samapattih* is with an object's word, meaning, and knowledge.

Any word is a doorway. Words will try at best to lead somewhere special in the wilderness of our consciousness. They're not always accurate, and their precision is always codependent on the context of the listener.

Patanjali's word is *samapattih*, or enlightenment. Which is, and should be, a very foreign concept to us when we first delve into the art of conscious liberation. It begins only as a word. Its promise is seemingly unrealistic fantasia. For most, it's considered rhetoric of an ancient world devoid of scientific evaluation. But to the very few who have, for just a short moment, taken the time to separate themselves from the inertia of their lives, to meditate, will have noticed that that meaningful pause they discovered is just the very beginning of something practical and inciteful.

This career of developing awareness begins with just a simple word. And that word leads to an *artha*, or meaning. We infer that enlightenment is conscious liberation. We define it as being things like pure awareness, an original perception, a place without cause and effect. All of these varied ideas weigh on the experience of the word's listener. Have they had an experience of pure awareness yet? Do they maintain a daily practice and have an illustrative idea of their perception's ebb and flow? These experiences are the real definition to the word *samapattih*. Patanjali can only show us the door. Now it's entirely up to us to match the world he alludes to with our own experience.

Which leads us to *jñāna*, or knowledge. An architecture designed by both experience and context. Our experiences culminate in the real definition of a word. But unlike objective words such as a cat or a dog, words that describe conscious awareness such as *samapattih* are refering to the pointing itself, not the object. It's a lot easier to describe a cat than it is the medium of awareness. But the best way to define either is to familiarize yourself with their experience.

Text 1.43

स्मृतिपरिशुद्धौ स्वरूपशून्येवार्थमात्रनिर्भासा निर्वितर्का
smṛti-pariśuddhau svarūpa-śūnyeva-arthamātra-nirbhāsā nirvitarkā

smṛti	Memory
pariśuddhau	Purging
svarūpa	Of its own nature
śūnya	Without, empty
iva	Like
artha	Meaning, picture
mātra	Only
nirbhāsā	Without darkness
nirvitarkā	Without physical awarenesss

The second layer of *samapattih*, is when memory is purified, and the mind is left absent of its own nature, and all that is left is the object illuminated without mental discrimination.

The patterned mind will label everything it touches based on the coincidence of its patterns. It will never, however, label what the world actually is, because the world is, and will always be, more expansive than a mind can understand. In this case, the word is *samapattih*, and even with its curt definition *total absorption*, we will each individually have an infinite number of descriptions of what that experience is and what it means.

Patanjali writes that to truly understand the word, or any word for that matter, we must first purify our memory. Essentially, remove ourselves from our past and stare at the world as if this word and the world around us are the first and only experience we have ever had. Going further, Patanjali also encourages us to completely remove ourselves from our nature. So instead of experiencing this phenomenon of a word as a you in particular, or even as a human or a even a living being, you should attempt to experience it as an awareness without a body, a time, or a place.

Eventually, the object, in this case the word *samapattih*, will finally be able to exist without your ego's dangerous scalpels of discrimination. Should the ego become involved with any definition whether it's a word, or a friendship, a city, or a pasttime, it will always define that word in relation to how it empowers that ego. By completely removing ourselves from such an ego, that *artha* or word will be able to reveal itself as itself with no strings attached.

Text 1.44

एतयैव सविचारा निर्विचारा च सूक्ष्मविषय व्याख्याता

etayaiva savicārā nirvicārā ca sūkṣma-viṣaya vyākhyātā

etayā	By this
eva	Like
savicārā	With subtle awareness
nirvicārā	Beyond awareness
ca	And
sūkṣma	Subtle
viṣaya	Object of the senses
vyākhyātā	Are described

The third and fourth layer of samapattih is through our subtle awareness, and then finally the absence of our awareness.

From the very beginning, there are so many vectors deciding our direction. They are an unconscious puppeteer to our daily lives. The more obvious vectors are our hunger, our sexual interests, or our limitless thirst for distraction. However, once we reconcile those needs, and pursue something more valuable, something more long-term and meaningful, the vectors then puppeteer ourselves towards goals such as developing a stronger social circle, a healthier body, or advancing our careers.

Every subtle reaction we have, every choice we make, every step we take is formatted by the interests of these vectors. The vectors are defined by our conscious awareness, and then we politely run on their autopilot.

In this sutra, Patanjali describes the absolute purification of these vectors. When our conscious awareness can completely extinguish our patterned thought, removing ourselves entirely from our individual sense of awareness. From this sacred place, the vectors are rendered ineffectual. They no longer direct. They have no goal or interest. They become, just as your awareness becomes, a pure reflection of reality without the necessity of an observer.

Here in lies the most subtle of balances. To be human, we must maintain this body, and serve those around us. This requires us to dabble in karma. It requires us to play with a vector of some subtle individual interest. Patanjali's direction here is then to make these decisions as close as possible to the place of a directionless, empty vector. Use only enough effort of interest to think of cooking food for someone hungry, but nothing more.

The word is *samapattih*, and to even approach it's meaning, we must use the least amount of effort so that we don't separate it from its truth.

Text 1.45

सूक्ष्मविषयत्वम्चालिण्ग पर्यवसानम्

sūkṣma-viṣayatvam-ca-aliṇga paryavasānam

sūkṣma	Subtle
viṣaya	Object of the senses
ca	And
aliṅga	Without a sign
paryavasānam	Concluding, extending to

Once you observe the subtle, you can follow this observation to its source, to the unmanifest origin of all things.

The lifespan of a moment exists only in our awareness. And when our awareness fades, our presence dies, and our mental faculties take over. But this mind is only a thirdhand presence. It works as the cheap generic brand of presence that comes with the caveat of a delusional memory, and limited to only human senses. So not only do we experience a fraction of what the world is through our limited senses, but we only vaguely remember them.

Should we hold on to any memory, then that presence ages. And before long, we are succumbed in a baseless emotion, standing in a place that never existed. When we let presence decay like this, we are left alone in a world to ourselves. Free from the boundaries of a reality shared by others. We are given the privilege of tweaking and modifying this delusionary myriad of details in a strategic chess move to position our ego so that all pieces revolve around us. This includes our awareness. Which means, no longer do we see the forest around us, we only see the parts of the forest that at that time we believe serves us. A dangerous malady!

Just as there's an enormous value placed in knowing where our food comes from. The yogi equally considers the source of their memories and experiences. When having the experience of observing a bird, did the observation originate in pure awareness, or did their observeration originate as the yogi being an individual with an individual name seeing a bird? If it was the latter, then their source was contaminated, and they were likely only seeing themselves regardless of what they were looking at. Because the observer had a name, and an identity, they were not present. The experience was delusional. And is, for the most part, worthless to someone who wants to see the world around them and not just entertain their ego.

Patanjali describes here the importance of source. Know your memories' source. Know the source of your conscious awareness. The purity of a feeling, a choice, a friend, literally anything we perceive -- is how close you can posture ourselves to the source of pure awareness while minimally being aware of that object. Anymore more than the minimum is ego.

Text 1.46

ता एव सबीजस्समाधिः
tā eva sabījas-samādhiḥ

tā	They [four states of
eva	samāpattiḥ]
sabīja	Also
samādhiḥ	With seed
	Pure equanimity of consciousness, the goal of yoga

These four meditations are the only perceptions with an object as their seed.

Each of these samadhis begin with a seed that leads you to their source. As a thread helps the lost traveler through a labyrinth , each one leading to the next. The first state of *samāpattiḥ* is a word and its knowledge. The second is the world behind the cloud of discriminative thought. The third and fourth are the extremely subtle apparati of awareness. Tools only available to someone who abandons being someone.

Now, lets think of those four states backwards now. Just as that original word led us to the state pure awareness. You could also say that vice versa, there is a *samskara* of awareness within us that lead us to the word. We began with pure awareness, unadulterated and truthful except one very small little flaw. The flaw is an almost unnoticeable apparati in our consciousness that reacts to an experience between a self and a phenomenon. That experience leads us to a rationalization without thought, and finally that experience leads us to a knowledge and its respective words.

The path back and forth are identified in the Yoga Sutras as with seeds or *sabīja*. There is a something to hold on to. A very specific rope to guide us back and forth through the maze.

Text 1.47

निर्विचारवैशारद्येऽध्यात्मप्रसादः
nirvicāra-vaiśāradye-'dhyātma-prasādaḥ

nirvicārā	Without subtle thoughts, superreflective
vaiśāradye	Undisturbed clarity
adhyātma	Of the absolute soul
prasādaḥ	Lucidity

When we can master our most subtle nature with undisturbed clarity, our true self reveals itself.

Every nuance of perception influences our life. They lead us like the fingers of a puppeteer. Most of the time we're unaware of how scripted our lives are by these influences. The aid is practicing non-attachment, which will lead us past our gross impulses, our logic, past our feelings, until all that is left is the object of focus and the illusion of perceiver.

Non-attachment or *vairagya* leads us to the last thread of disconnection between the world that is and the illusion of self. One experiences a dance between total non-duality and the faint whisper of a so-called self. The clarity of witnessing the borders of these two realms illustrates why we interpret a God or *Isvara*, how the origin of material matter or *prakirti* evolves, or how the universal consciousness or *purusha* is shared and expressed by all living beings.

But most importantly, it illuminates why consciousness leads to suffering. The negotiation between this last thread of a self and the world as it is reveals those who suffer. As common as we believe suffering is, we rarely notice how almost every living experience is tailored around an inability to address that pain.

Text 1.48

ऋतंभरा तत्र प्रज्ञा

ṛtaṁbharā tatra prajñā

ṛtam	Truth
bharā	Bearing
tatra	There
prajñā	Pure wisdom

That experience of elevated cognition is where wisdom comes from.

The mind is not capable of being conscious. It is simply a tool. We use it to survive. Whether the mind is adept and accurate or dull and incognizant, there is no difference to our conscious awareness. You can be illiterate and brain-damaged but be consciously aware as much as you could with a mind that is versed in sacred texts and that has the focus to meditate for weeks on end.

That said, it is imperative to understand that there is a very sincere difference between a truth bearing wisdom and a truth bearing awareness. This sutra refers to a truth bearing wisdom. But the mind's wisdom is merely a temporary echo and ocassionally does not reflect a perfect awareness.

Sometimes our truth bearing wisdom is a product of hard studying, listening to great teachers, memorizing beautiful texts, or surrounding ourselves with perfect environments. That does not, however, mean that those positive influences have broken all the way through to our soul or *atma* and burned up our latent impressions.

We have not yet become a source of wisdom. We are still, at this state, only an echo of it. We might be close, but change any one of those attributes; remove us from our environment, remove our ability to memorize a sacred text, remove the proximity of our favorite teacher, and we may come to the realization that our progress along the path is a lot more tedious than we imagined.

Text 1.49

श्रुतानुमानप्रज्ञाअभ्यामन्यविषया विशेषार्थत्वात्

śruta-anumāna-prajñā-abhyām-anya-viṣayā viśeṣa-arthatvāt

śruta	That which is heard
anumāna	Inferred
prajñā	Wisdom
anya	Other
viṣayā	Object of the senses
viśeṣa	Special
artha	Meaning
arthatvāt	As its object, in relation to

True knowledge is knowledge unaffilated with logic. Testimony and reasoning are separate from true knowledge because they are dependent on a specific object.

Knowledge without form is eternal. But when we apply a dialect to it, then its wisdom will only last as long as its dialect is still understood. The greatest wisdom has no words or specific object to describe it with. By not gift-wrapping truth in words, truth is suddenly accessible to all beings. When presence alone defines truth, then even the smallest ant can lead you on the spiritual Path.

Text 1.50

तज्जस्संस्कारोऽन्यसंस्कार प्रतिबन्धी
tajjas-saṁskāro-'nya-saṁskāra pratibandhī

tad	This
ja	Born of, from
saṁskāra	Deep latent impressions in consciousness
anya	Other, different
saṁskāra	Instincts, reactions
pratibandhī	Obstruct, prevent

Any experience of knowledge will drown out lesser knowledges.

Our experiences design us. Every experience leaves an imprint. When we suffer, we echo that suffering for quite some time. When we love, we echo that love for quite some time. However, in the rare opportunity that an experience leads us to awareness, that particular imprint will outshine all other experiences. Awareness by itself is essentially a greater experience than anything else in particular.

That's because awareness elevates all other experiences. What's greater than your favorite food? Being aware of eating your favorite food. What's greater than love? Being aware of that love. The more we have this unique experience of awareness, the more we realize how much more valuable it is than whatever it is we happen to be experiencing.

As Jesus once said, 'what do you benefit if you gain the whole world but lose your soul'? Your experiences are the world. They come and go, and are at best only beneficial to only a temporary body. Your soul, however, is the awareness. It is eternal.

To understand this awareness, we have to understand that this awareness isn't actually a part of 'the you'. It is an awareness that occurs before the senses distort your perception. It's an awareness that occurs even before the mind does. It happens before you do.

More simply, you could imagine yourself as a software that awareness uses. Whatever you call yourself is just the program. But you you yourself can not be aware by yourself. Just as computer software can not be aware by itself. It can function and perform all sorts of complicated maths, but it is not conscious. Just as it is unrealistic to say, "*I* am aware". It's more accurate to say, "I am allowing awareness to pass through me." The 'I' is only a humble extension of a greater awareness.

Anything less than this awareness will hinder your path. It will become a spiritual dead end. An abstraction of a so called 'peace' is a dead end. An abstraction of 'love' is a dead end. But if you value your awareness above all else, you will be lead to a sacred place before the world is.

Text 1.51

तस्यापि निरोधे सर्वनिरोधान्निर्बीजः समाधिः
tasyāpi nirodhe sarva-nirodhān-nirbījaḥ samādhiḥ

tasyaapi	And this also
nirodhe	Upon cessation
sarva	Of everything, from
nirodhat	everything
nirbījaḥ samādhiḥ	From cessation
	Seedless enlightenment,
	enlightenment without cause

And when this last truth-bearing samskara recedes, we are left with causeless liberation.

In this last sutra we find the end. It is the door. Patanjali can not take us through this door. He can, at best, only describe its design, how it works, how it was made, but its passage is beyond commentary. It is beyond reason.

It is the last token of realization we will have before the road ends and so do we. Beyond this point, something will still go on, but we won't. It is the top of the mountain. And at the top of this mountain, it is said only Lou Tzou's slippers were found.

The door also marks the end of the practice that brought you there. Every great teaching is a vehicle. But when we reach the other side, we can go no further until we also abandon the vehicle. Just as the Buddha abandon's his raft after reaching the other shore.

Thus so far, we've learned that the path to this door is loving awareness. An awareness that presents itself as greater than the self. Up to this point, Patanjali has described several techniques and a means of perception that cultivate this practice of awareness. It can also be referred to as *nirodha-samskara*, a destroyer of all *samskaras*. It is the last samskara. *Nirodha-samskara* is still a samskara even though it is one that eliminates other *samskaras*. But it is the last as well as the doorway to our origin. Beyond it, is a sacred place called *nirbījaḥ samādhiḥ* or seedless enlightenment. This means there is no cause or force working against this state. Nothing brings us there.

As such, nothing will ever again move us from there. It is a place of no time nor space or reason of any kind.

It should be noted that in other traditions such as Gaudiya-Vaisnavism, this door is humbly never approached. The Vaisnav seeks transcendental enlightenment by serving God as two separate entities, the devotee and the devoted. The door to them is God incarnate, and their teaching is based on celebrating the love and humility of their separation rather than becoming one with such a being. Were they even offered the choice to enter such a door, they would joyfully refuse so they could continue serving their love. The Buddhists among the *Mahayana* sects believes in entering this door, but also in returning to this world to help others find it. This is called the vow of the *Bodhisattva*. That one's enlightenment is never fulfilled until everyone else is.

Patanjali offers you no preference. He merely describes its existence, and how to find it.

Chapter Two

Text 2.1

तपः स्वाध्यायेश्वरप्रणिधानानि क्रियायोगः

tapaḥ svādhyāy-eśvarapraṇidhānāni kriyā-yogaḥ

tapaḥ	Austerity, discipline
svādhyāya	Self-awareness
īśvarapraṇidhāna	Unconditional service, submission to God
kriyā	Action, movement towards
yogaḥ	Yoga

The movement towards yoga requires austerity, self-awareness, and unconditional service.

If yoga means effortless origin, than it would be paradoxical to say you're *doing yoga*. What's there to do if no effort exists? I believe this is why Patanjali prepends the word with *kriyā* meaning action, or action that leads towards yoga, our effortless origin.

The three prerequisites, Patanjali describes, act as both the consequence of this effortless origin as well as the pathway to it. In the same way, you could say one can become love by loving just as you could say one is loving because they are love. Austerity, self-awareness, and unconditional service are both the cause and consequence of being true to nature.

Tapasya is a taste or an interest in a greater context. To understand *tapasya*, think of the houseplant that will only ever grow as large as its pot. The pot is the context from which we view the world. If we judge the world based on our financial success, then we will have a financial-sized pot. If we judge the world based on power, then we have a power-sized pot. But if we judge the world based on transcendence beyond the material world, then there is no longer a pot nor a limit to our growth. This elevated taste is a prerequisite to move beyond the animal-like instincts we have to fight or run from the world around us.

We could meditate for years on end, but if we never acquire a taste for a higher context, the practice will create someone who is overqualified for the position, but who lacks the interest to ever apply for the job. The job is *svādhyāya*, or self-awareness. It is a process of examining this *tapasyah* within the context of our actions, our emotions, and the source of our inspiration. How do they compare? *Tapasyah* is the blueprint for a garden. *Svādhyāya* is the act of gardening. And in this act of gardening, we rigorously check between the context of a higher consciousness and movement of our spirit, mind, and body.

This garden will inevitably bear fruit. Your practice will make you smarter, healthier, attractive, and well known. But these benefits will also inevitably destroy the truth of your message. Because these fruits are not yours. You are merely its messenger. *Iśvarapraṇidhāna* is the service to this origin. It is the highest practice. It is when the yogi returns the fruit right back to the Earth it came from.

Text 2.2

समाधिभावनार्थः क्लेश तनूकरणार्थश्च
samādhi-bhāvana-arthaḥ kleśa tanū-karaṇa-arthaś-ca

samādhi	Enlightened consciousness
bhāvana	Developing towards, aligned
arthaḥ	with
kleśa	For the purpose of, a goal
tanū	Afflictions
karaṇa	Weak
	To achieve, to make

And this is for the purpose of minimizing illusive reality to bring about enlightenment.

Offering space is a simple act. A mother is naturally talented in this. She reenacts it anytime her child loses her favorite toy and a category five temper tantrum emerges. The mother doesn't encourage the storm nor deny the child its pain – she simply responds with a loving indifference, and allows the *karma* to subside. The same way a therapist will simply listen. They will never encourage your suffering nor deny you your pain. The result is the trauma or *karma* has a chance to run its course. Simply offer space for your suffering to exist, and these things too shall pass.

The next step is to extend that mother's gift of compassion and extend it to the whole of reality. Why is it easier for a mother to accept her child, but challenging when having to accept the world? The answer lies within context. For the novice practitioner, they strictly serve the child. But as the context broadens, we soon realize that there are no boundaries to this so-called child. Society, the streets, and the passing birds are also the child. Watching society wrestle over race issues and corporate greed is also the child. And with a mother's grace, we should approach all of these circumstances with that same loving comfort – neither encouraging the storm nor denying the child its pain.

This is the process of ending *kleśam* or obstacles. Should we respond in any other way, they are guaranteed to return. And when they stop returning, the path towards mental freedom materializes.

Text 2.3

अविद्याअस्मितारागद्वेषाभिनिवेशः क्लेशाः
avidyā-asmitā-rāga-dveṣa-abhiniveśaḥ kleśāḥ

avidyā	Ignorance
asmitā	Self-centeredness, attached to that which is changing
rāga	Attachment
dveṣa	Aversion
abhiniveśaḥ	Fear of death, a will to live
kleśaḥ	Impediments, burdens

There are five kinds of obstacles; ignorance, ego, addiction, aversion, and a fear of death.

Patanjali beautifully describes here the process of how materialism spreads like a disease throughout the spiritual body. In a perfect order no less; ignorance, ego, addiction, aversion, and death. Each layer leading to the origin, definition, and architecture of suffering.

First, there is *ignorance*. We forget that our consciousness is inherent among all beings. We forget that there is no actual difference between any human being, animal, fish, or plant. Because of this ignorance, we are able to carve an illusion of self from an illusion of world.

Second, these two separate identities are called *ego*. This leads us to believe that this newfound identity is somehow unique. Ego convinces us that our experience in life is somehow separate.

Third, now that there is both a separate 'me' that has a something, an ego, we quickly find *attachment*. This separation identity gives us the taste of power like blood to a wolf. We become ravenous to continue the inertia of a me. I am, while the world is not. We begin serving the body more than the soul.

And that clinging leads us to *aversion*. Nothing in actual reality can sustain this bizarre complex of materialism besides our imagination. Therefore, we become aversive to anything that doesn't fulfill this imaginary individuality. We become aversive to those poorer than us, less educated than us, less spiritual than us; we fantasize feelings of disgust so we can separate us further from reality, and perpetuate the I.

Lastly, we acquire a *fear of death*. Which means that the illusion of self has gone beyond the layer of just a craving. In death, we're up against losing this beautiful composition of cravings. We admire the innumerable choices of our brief individuality. Just as an ocean's wave might for one brief moment praise its rise above the rest. We defend this sandcastle ego, it's unique choices, friendships, and devotion. It is, in the eye of the wave, incapable of seeing the ocean. And so a fear arises. Simply, because we forgot that we were never separate. We forgot that we are still the ocean.

Text 2.4

अविद्या क्षेत्रमुत्तरेषाम् प्रसुप्ततनुविच्छिन्नोदाराणाम्
avidyā kṣetram-uttareṣām prasupta-tanu-vicchinn-odārāṇām

avidyā	Ignorance
kṣetram	Field
uttareṣām	Other ones, next ones
prasupta	Dormant
tanu	Weak
vicchinnā	Broken, interrupted
udāranam	Is powerful from all of this

Forgetting your nature is the breeding ground for spiritual obstacles. These obstacles come in four states : dormant, weakened, interrupted, and active.

In Western thought, we reserve the word 'addiction' to very obvious patterns like drugs and alcohol, chocolate or neuroticism. But around 400 BCE, addiction was identified as all patterns, regardless of whether they were harmful or even noticeable. Every addiction begins at the split moment when we slip from the brink of pure presence. Whether it's a passing thought, or something distracting you, the moment you lose your breath to anything other than presence, an addiction is born.

We call this ignorance or *avidyā*. Our most common mistake with addiction is to think that a particular thing like chocolate, or drugs, or sex was the addiction. Really our addiction begins at the moment of losing our presence. When our life experience becomes predictable. So simple and predictable, that we can repeat it. Over and over again just like a drug. Even though life is, in all actuality entirely unpredictable, we figure out a way to consume a complacent unchanging variant of it. This loss of presence or *avidyā*, is what leads us to a lifetime of prewritten patterns.

These prewritten patterns, formed from ignorance, come in four layers. *Udāranam* or active patterns are things that are actively driving your ideas and movements. They are very common habits to you. They puppeteer your emotional responses and are essentially your identity's autopilot. *Vicchinnā* or interrupted patterns are patterns with the same force but because of the distance you put between you and them, you have liberated yourself temporarily. These are habits you have not yet formerly canonized because you likely don't experience them too often. The only thing that prevents them from becoming *udāranam* is the frequency of their use. *Tanu* or weakened patterns are those that, over time, have diminished. They still steal your breath and focus but to a lesser extent. Just like an old craving you've consciously begun walking away from. *Prasupta* or dormant patterns are those you do not notice, but still exist. They are waiting for the perfect environment to grow again. And so we slip through these four layers, back and forth, puppeteered by their relative strengths. The idea is that once we can reduce a pattern to its dormant state through meditation we can there burn the pattern entirely so that it may never grow again. A life without pattern is enlightenment.

Text 2.5

अनित्याअशुचिदुःखानात्मसु नित्यशुचिसुखाअत्मख्यातिरविद्या
anityā-aśuci-duḥkha-anātmasu nitya-śuci-sukha-ātmakhyātir-avidyā

anitya	Temporal, transitory
aśuci	Impure
duḥkha	Pain, suffering
anātmasu	The non true self
nitya	Eternal, immortal
śuci	Pure, clean
sukha	Joy, happiness
ātma	The self's soul
khyāti	Perception, insight
avidyā	Ignorance

The first obstacle and catalyst is ignorance which leads to confusing the transient as eternal, the impure as pure, suffering as happiness, and the ego as the soul.

We were once a simple organism. We were barely separate from any ordinary mineral or molecule. Through countless species, after millions of years, our sense of survival designed us a pair of eyes. And as such, a seer was designed as well. And now our survival is perhaps longer, but our separation is greater.

That's because eyes were designed to see only what serves survival. They were not designed for self-awareness. Hearing, taste, and touch as well were all naturally designed to sense what serves survival. They do not sense self-awareness.

The mind was also designed by survival. The mind doesn't understand awareness because the mind is just like the eyes, unaware. The mind is simply a tool of our awareness. Therefore, it will only perform to the limits of self-survival. Anything beyond survival wasn't written in the mind's User Manual.

This is where the confusion arises. If all we had was access to this mind and these senses then we would experience a life based on survival not one of conscious awakening. We would inevitably confuse the impermanent for the permanent, the impure for the pure, and suffering for happiness. Because we can only see, feel, hear, taste, touch, and think about a self that is trying to survive. That's what we were designed to do.

But awareness was designed to be aware. And for a few of us, we may have caught a glimpse of what this awareness is. We may have observed something being aware through this body, our senses, and ultimately the mind. And if we follow that awareness – if we leave behind all this nonsense survivalism -- what we end up finding is an eternal, pure happiness.

Text 2.6

दृग्दर्शनशक्त्योरेकात्मतैवास्मिता

dr̥g-darśana-śaktyor-ekātmata-iva-asmitā

dr̥k	The seeing self
darśana-śakti	The power of sight
ekatmata	One soul, one nature
eva	As if
asmitā	Ego

The second obstacle is ego which is confusing pure awareness for your self's awareness.

There is only one being that shines a light through every life. Our lives are windows of that light. Ego is a thread of ignorance that arises when we confuse this light with this temporary body, and our life's work. It's not ignorant to claim a name and act in the world. But it is ignorant to lose the context that this name, and these actions are shockwaves of a much greater name, and a far greater action.

To make sense of this, we must realize that our individual awareness is secondhand to the origin of awareness. Our individual awareness is composed of many tools of perception; eyes, nose, ears, a mind, and an entire hormonal system sending millions of subtle messages. All of this composes an individual awareness. Which gives us a great sense of survivalism, but a minimalist sense of greater awareness. Instead of being aware of the world outside of ourselves, we become very distracted by the magical phenomena of our individualist awareness.

This is the birth of ego. The illusive duality that stands convinced that there is something different between greater awareness and its extension, individual awareness. Just as if your right hand was suddenly convinced it was an individual, and independent of the body. That it was moving on its own volition. Our ego professes that we are a living being is somehow separate from awareness. The same awareness that moves through all living and non-living beings.

It's important to note that the tools themselves are not aware. Makes them come alive. Just as you can make a hammer come alive by using it. But the hammer by itself has no awareness. Our body and mind equally has no awareness. Our entire being is simply an extension of an original consciousness. An awareness that exists before we do.

Text 2.7

सुखानुशयी रागः

sukha-anuśayī rāgaḥ

sukha	Joy, good fortune
anuśayī	The consequence of
rāga	Attachment

Attachment depends on pleasure.

We forget who we are. We adopt the ego. We become separated. We become an illusive so-called self who is somehow different from this illusive so-called world. This separation is as unstable as it is imaginative. It cannot last.

Every single passing moment is a threat to its existence. Every single detail in life is proof that there is no border between you and this world. That's a very hard pill to swallow for an ego. And that is where attachment comes in.

Attachment is the architecture that supports this separation. The harder we cling, the less likely we will see the world and think we are apart of it. This attachment is a powerful tool to the ego. It works as a guard against silence. In those precious moments when we are available to listen that connection; to someone or something – attachment will fill such a lovely experience with a cacophony of meaningless thought.

This train of thought usually goes something like this : I am this unique individual with individual ideas. This source of individualism is far more captivating then the world my ideas come from. I will ignore this world so that I can make more time for this self.

Before long, this 'individuality' becomes an echo chamber of the same idea repeating over and over again. It is a power mantra. One that will help us survive, but it will never make us aware. We will become only aware of our self. We'll very soon forget about the people around us. We'll forget the welfare of our environment. We will barely recognize the suffering caused from eating meat.

The ego maintains itself with the joy of its own echo.

Text 2.8

दुःखानुशयी द्वेषः
duḥkha-anuśayī dveṣaḥ

duḥkha	Suffering
anuśayī	The consequence of
dveṣaḥ	Aversion

Aversion comes from suffering.

Our consciousness is just like a home among the woods. It makes its best attempt to stand alone, but not for long. The consciousness may have the boundaries of a unique personality, likes and dislikes, but not for long. It is at every moment, just as every element born from nature, being tempted back into the greater awareness it was born from. One day, the forest will reclaim the home.

We fight against this. We fight against the whole of nature to remain something separate. We fight with our blood, our sweat, and our tears to prevent such an inevitable return. Just as a home among the woods attempts to hold itself up and against the hunger of the forest.

We call this aversion. It comes in different forms. Sometimes it's anger. Sometimes it's hatred. But we can safely say that all aversion is fear, and all fear is born from pain. Not just any kind of pain. It is born from a pain we endure without knowing. A mother will endure incalculable pain during childbirth. But that doesn't necessarily stop her from wanting to do it again. That's because she knows the pain's value. There is a knowing. As long as there's knowing, fear won't take root.

However, if someone loses a friend, or their job, or someone hurts them – it's trickier to find value in such a tragic experience. It's harder to have a knowing. These kinds of experiences, without knowing, become aversion and fear. They become anger. They become hatred. They very easily become bigotry and racism.

All of which keep us rigorously motivated to maintain these homes among the woods. We hack at the tangling vines, we chemically treat the wood, we dump pounds of herbicide to the four corners of the property. We bleach everything inside and out. If we have to, we'll burn the forest down.

But truth be told, the forest was always us. It is us. We were never separate. The reason why we're scared is because we simply havn't accepted this. Knowing that we are already this nature, this forest, will open up a world of acceptance for our suffering. It may not cure the pain, but it allows us to understand it. And as such, it won't become fear. We won't become fear. When fear doesn't puppeteer, conscious awareness comes through. We witness a purer awareness.

Fear is the fourth obstacle in our spiritual path. It is born from suffering without wisdom.

Text 2.9

स्वरस्वाहि विदुषोऽपि समारूढोऽभिनिवेशः
svarasvāhi viduṣo-'pi samārūḍho-'bhiniveśaḥ

sva	Own
rasa	Potency, essence
vāhī	Carrying, bearing
viduṣa	Possessor of wisdom, guru
api	Even
samā	Fully, equally
rūdhaḥ	Established, dominating
abhiniveśaḥ	Fear of death, will to live

Even the most learned practitioners are equally rooted in the fear of death and change.

It's difficult to hear the crickets, observe a flock of birds, or flip through a collection of vintage photos and convince ourselves we were once them. There's something uncomfortable about not seeing in others all the effort we've placed into our own particular life. In the eyes of a wild animal, we don't see our humor, our language, our friends or family. They don't know them. The wildlife, the trees, the strangers in the subway do not know our secrets nor our memories. They do not know the things that are sometimes the only reason we wake up in the morning. We might be suicidal if those things were taken from us. That's why most of us don't see ourselves in others. We would lose the will to live if we were anything else. Instead we draw a very strict wall between this self and others. A wall designed by our attachment to the things that make us unique and individual.

But the yogi chips away at this wall. Because if we strip those things away, allowing ourselves to live for something deeper than our things and relationships, what we find is a very real and common thread we share with all beings. We find the will to be aware, to realize the self, and to serve. We find the nature of awareness.

When we live for this awareness alone rather than our identity, we suddenly see ourselves in all living beings. We are the ancient peoples, the strangers at the bus stop, and the animals among the brush. Each of us as one series of lives strung together by our persuit to serve our origin. This is called rebirth. One life after another, exploring the boundaries of our awareness. Each of us, individually, exploring our nature.

The fear of death and of change is the last of the five *kleśaḥ* or distractions towards our path. This distraction is the fruit of the prior four. It is a wall designed by ignorance, ego, attachment, and aversion. When those four coalesce we no longer see this rebirth. We no longer see ourselves in others. And as such, death seems permanent. But if we did see rebirth, if we saw this self among all living beings, we suddenly realize immortality isn't some foreign or strange concept. Death would no longer distract us.

Text 2.10

ते प्रतिप्रसवहेयाः सूक्ष्माः
te pratiprasava-heyāḥ sūkṣmāḥ

te	These [five kleśaḥ]
pratiprasavam	Return to their origin
heya	To overcome, eliminate
sūkṣmāḥ	Subtle

These five distractions devolve, become subtle, and are eliminated as the consciousness returns to its origin.

There is a beaten path between truth and unreality. Truth being our origin, our nature, and our peace. Unreality being our confusion and megalomania. We've all witnessed people on both spectrums. We've witnessed people walk back and forth on this path for better and for worse.

The path between both worlds is in five simple steps. From the side of truth, it begins with ignorance (*avidya*) and forgetting who we are. This leads to developing an ego (*asmitā)* and the belief that we are something unique and different from the world we live in. Attachment (*rāga*) inevitably develops by the sheer inertia of this process. Aversion (*dveṣaḥ*) maintains this separation. And finally, the fear of death and change (*abhiniveśaḥ*) is its unwillingness to look back or return.

There is so much gravity on the side of nonreality. People who have crossed over in this direction carry with them resentment towards mindfulness. They are the ones who have no time for meditation, but all the time in the world for a nervous breakdown. Even the idea of taking time to meditate is repulsive. This is their *abhiniveśaḥ*, their fear of change protesting against the unlimited medicine they are surrounded by.

Let's try the other way now. If they can swallow a little fear, and be open to the idea of change, they can approach the things they run from (*abhiniveśaḥ*). They can question them. Usually none of them can answer why they are averse to a breathing practice. Perhaps it makes them uncomfortable, but it's not necessarily a deal breaker. They decide to tiptoe past their aversions (*dveṣaḥ*). They sit.

They observe their attachments. It generally takes some time, maybe years, but one day they will realize that their attachments never really represented them at all (*rāga*). The practice has in some powerful way transcended their superfluous needs. Eventually, they realize that without superfluous desires, there's nothing separating themselves from anything else (*asmitā)*. They become aware of the emotional and spiritual state the trees and air have shared since the origin of time (*avidya*).

Now we've arrived back at truth. I wouldn't say there's gravity on this side of truth because nothing holds us there. But once we're there long enough, we'll find the path that lead us there will overgrow with flowering vines.

Text 2.11

ध्यान हेयाः तद्वृत्तयः
dhyāna heyāḥ tad-vṛttayaḥ

dhyāna	Meditation
heyāḥ	To avoid, eliminate
tad	Their [five kleśaḥ]
vṛttayaḥ	Thought waves

Meditation will weaken and destroy all of these five distractions.

If you step back from a fight, you'll understand the argument. If you stand on top of a mountain, you'll understand what surrounds you. If you listen to everyone's story, you'll understand history. Each of these is an example of expanding the context. Enlightenment should be seen as a synonym for context. Those who pursue enlightenment are those who pursue a greater context.

Meditation expands context. A child's context is based around simple appeals to survive. A child generally expects everyone and everything in its life to revolve around its own survival. As we grow older, we recognize that other peculiar beings just like ourselves exist outside of us. We develop an act of service to them. This happens because our context expanded.

But meditation goes deeper. Because even the awareness of others is obfuscated by illusions of ego and difference. Meditation takes a stab at withdrawing the player's glued eyes from the television screen to observe the controls in their hands. The context becomes not just the life we play, but also the awareness of the controls that give life.

What are my intentions? Why am I overwhelmed? What meaning is there in our life? All of these questions are perfectly solved by simply taking a moment away from the game to observe its engineering. Meditation answers them by asking a larger contextual questions. Why are you looking? Who is being overwhelmed? Where are the borders of this life?

Just as we discussed in the previous sutra, ignorance carries a gravity and an inertia to it. It will never feel good to look outside of ignorance. Our ego knows that pursuing truth will not serve it. So in order to find true awareness, we will need a raft that is greater than what serves us.

Text 2.12

क्लेशमूलः कर्माशयो दृष्टादृष्टजन्मवेदनीयः
kleśa-mūlaḥ karma-aśayo dr̥ṣṭa-adr̥ṣṭa-janma-vedanīyaḥ

kleśa	Impediments, obstacles
mūlaḥ	Root
karma	Cause and effect, physics
aśayaḥ	Tendencies, deposit
dr̥ṣṭa	Seen
adr̥ṣṭa	Unseen
janma	Birth
vedanīyaḥ	To experience

The root of illusive perception is stored in streams of consciousness that propagate into our thoughts and actions, some seen, some unseen, throughout all our births.

Our untold futures hide themselves across the consciousness like seeds among a forest. They are unawakened experiences. Some of these experiences were never yours, but your parents or your ancestors handed down to you either genetically or emotionally. They wait for an opportunity to incubate and give birth through your body, speech, and inspiration. Once we understand how these seeds of inspiration hatch, we become their designer rather than their echo.

Text 2.13

सति मूले तद्विपाको जात्यायुर्भोगाः
sati mūle tad-vipāko jāty-āyur-bhogāḥ

sati	When in existence, to be
mūle	there
tat	Root
vipāka	Whose
jāti	Outcome, fruit
āyuḥ	Caste, birth, quality
bhogāḥ	Life span
	Happiness, joy

Existing in this fertile mind, we find our seedling inspiration resting beneath our subconscious, at the root. These seedlings are composed of an event, a duration, and an effect.

Every seed of karma comes with an intention, a length of time it intends to last for, and an essence it intends to leave behind. But just like every seed, they are completely dependent on the environment they grow within.

Imagine your life as a karma garden. Your experiences, your dreams, the things you hear -- are all the flowers, trees, and riveting vines growing in this garden. Among them are the flowers that distract you. While there are others that allow you to be you as you are. What grows in the forest is inevitable. What survives in the forest depends on the ecosystem.

That ecosystem is composed of first your body, its health and intuition. But further its the people you surround yourself with, the intention you carry, the intention of others you witness, the architecture of the buildings you live within, the sound of traffic, and the way you water all this phenomena into the garden of your very heart.

Ask yourself, how do you maintain this karma garden?

Text 2.14

ते ह्लाद परितापफलाः पुण्यापुण्यहेतुत्वात्

te hlāda paritāpa-phalāḥ puṇya-apuṇya-hetutvāt

te	It
hlāda	Pleasure
paritāpa	Pain
phalāḥ	Outcome, fruits
puṇya	Virtue
apuṇya	Vice
hetutvāt	As a result

Those who take birth, experience pleasure and pain. Deeds caused by virtue or vice.

Trauma and love are emotional landscapes that move through generations, and can be seen anywhere from our languages to our cities. Our ancestor's emotional realization of life is passed hand over hand, generation after generation. In the context of a hundred thousand years, you can observe the emotional and spiritual evolution of a single soul among all life learning how to harmonize with itself and the world around.

This series of lives were all composed from trauma and love. We are living works of art. Bodies, languages, and music designed by tension and release, trauma and love, or, as Patanjali referred to it as, virtue and vice.

And from this meticulous design, we acquire the fruit of their respective pleasures and pains.

Text 2.15

परिणाम ताप संस्कार दुःखैः गुणवृत्तिविरोधाच्च दुःखमेव स
वं विवेकिनः

pariṇāma tāpa saṁskāra duḥkhaiḥ guṇa-vr̥tti-virodhācca
duḥkham-eva sarvaṁ vivekinaḥ

pariṇāma	Change, consequence
tāpas	Desire, distress
saṁskāra	Conscious imprints
duḥkhaiḥ	Sufferings, pains
guṇa	Of the three qualities of
vr̥tti	nature
virodhā	Thought patterns
ca	Conflict, resistance
duḥkham	And
eva	Sufferings, pains
sarvaṁ	Even, only
vivekinaḥ	Everything, all
	One who is discriminative

A wise person knows that all worldly experiences lead to suffering, and imprints in the consciousness.

Your entire life's experiences, your family, friends, and secret memories are all secondary experiences to their origin; which is love. Because they are secondary, if we dwell in them, those experiences recycle themselves karmically as thirdhand experiences, and fourth hand, and so on. Each one becoming a little less sincere than the last. A little further away from where it all began. A wise person doesn't dwell in the actions of their friends, themselves, or the world, but in the origin of these things. An origin that is also a state of mind, a sense of perception, and the cause of love.

If you pursue this origin in your breath and practice, you will eventually come to see a fountainhead called love. That even though we may be surrounded by ignorance and hatred, feel pain in times of great loss, we will realize that those experiences are not far from love. And that the way to solve that pain is simply by calling out to their origin. We realize that life isn't about dwelling in that pain, but holding it hand in hand, and returning with it to a home called love.

Text 2.16

हेयं दुःखमनागतम्
heyaṁ duḥkham-anāgatam

heyaṁ	To be avoided
duḥkham	Pain, suffering
anāgatam	Yet to come

Pain which is yet to arrive is prevented.

All action is the consequence of infinite repetition. A lot of things we will do and say today, are the result of thousands of generations before us, doing and saying the same thing. Over and over again. Each time it occurs, it perpetuates the action. You could say that the actions themselves are more alive than we are. You could say we are just the humble vessels for such sequences to pass through us.

When you see our lifetime as sustenance for an eternal action to pass through, it then becomes easy to see the many threads of intention around us. By studying history alone, we can see threads of hate, ignorance, love, betrayal, and pain pass through generation after generation, country to country. We are all inevitably reliving the same experiences, repeating the same mistakes, going through the same motions lifetime after lifetime.

This is where our breath becomes our greatest asset. Our breath becomes the vantage point to observe these various threads. From our breath, we can observe these infinite storm clouds of emotion, and repetitive consequence pass through us. Emotions that are as old as time, and have arrived to possess us from thousands of years ago. Yet knowing their origin and seeing their limited effect, we begin to see through these storms. We observe their origin instead of their immediate craze. We hold the heart instead of their mania. The pain they come packaged with can then be easily prevented.

But that pain is not avoided by rejecting or by hiding from these eternal threads of action. It comes from accepting their cause and understanding their craft. It comes from recognizing that these infinite threads of action, meticulously woven through each generation, are always secondary to love.

Love is the first. It is the beginning. From this origin all things manifest. All action occurs. Therefore every action will always be an abstraction of this original truth. Just as all things in this world are an abstraction of your true self.

So we look through the cloud, through the karma, through the daily routines, the hardships, and material success, to the kernel of truth. Our origin which is called love. That all things emenate from. We pursue that origin. We posture ourselves closer to it rather than its effect. And as such, pain is avoided.

Text 2.17

द्रष्टृदृश्ययोः संयोगो हेयहेतुः
draṣṭṛ-dṛśyayoḥ saṁyogo heyahetuḥ

draṣṭṛ	The seer
dṛśyaḥ	That which is seen
saṁyoga	Unity, conjunction
heya	To be avoided
hetuḥ	The cause

The original state of mind and that which we observe is a union to be avoided.

There is an awkward moment when you realize that the body is in the way. It is standing in between your awareness and the world you witness. It is, at best, only offering an obscure perception of the world. One riddled and confused by irrelevant needs, imagination, and fear. You could very easily simulate this experience by staring at your best friend through a kaleidoscope. You know fully well they are there, but your perception of them is hindered by a distracting psychedelic experience.

But we must make do. We can not witness without the body. So we make a compromise. The compromise is context. Instead of getting lost within the kaleidoscope, mesmerized by its infinite beauty, we recognize that our friend is something greater and beyond this splintered light. We recognize that the kaleidoscope is simply a tool. Just as we recognize the mind is just a tool. Both are quite exciting tools to use, but we must not confuse them with the awareness that uses them. The original awareness and the tool are two completely different things. Awareness and the mind is the same difference between you and the kaleidoscope. The trick is to hold such a wonderful tool to our eyes and not confuse our awareness with all the pretty colors.

The mind, our emotions, and this body are just an array of colorful tools. The best possible use of them is to operate them as a mirror. In this way, we can use them to gaze back at the awareness that uses them. Instead of using the mind to experience a virtual reality, we use the mind to recognize its owner, awareness. Instead of using the body for fleeting pleasures, we develop it with exercise and health to support a physical awareness. Instead of running away with the senses, we devote each one to the act of celebrating our truth.

And at the end of the day, we politely remind ourselves, we are not these tools. We are not the mind. We are not the body. We are not the senses. We are an eternal awareness. We are the unconditional yearning to love.

Whenever you suffer, no matter how great or small, it is because you have confused one for the other.

Text 2.18

प्रकाशक्रियास्थितिशीलं
भूतेन्द्रियाअत्मकं भोगापवर्गा
थं दृश्यम्

prakāśa-kriyā-sthiti-śīlaṁ bhūtendriya-ātmakaṁ bhoga-apavarga-arthaṁ dr̥śyam

prakāśa	Illumination
kriyā	Activity
sthiti	Remaining in a condition
śīla	Characteristics of
bhūta	Of the five elements
indriya	Senses
ātmakaṁ	Having the nature of
bhoga	Pleasure, life enjoyment
apavarga	Liberation
arthaṁ	Purpose
dr̥śyam	The seen, knowable

All existence originates from illumination, activity, and inertia. These energies compose the five elements, and are processed by the instruments of our senses. Their only purpose is to lead us to experience enlightenment.

We could spend years, if not, lifetimes rattling off about the descriptions of spiritual texts. We could write centuries of commentaries about what Jesus said, or how Buddha thought, or what Krishna meant, or why the Church of the Flying Spaghetti Monster makes sense. We could very easily get lost in this labyrinth of endless description – or we could describe their root energetic intention, and resolve the matter in seconds.

These roots are referred to as *gunas*. *Rajas*, *Tamas*, and *Sattva* which respectively describe movement, non-movement, and the illumination of both. All existence is composed of these three ingredients. From them, all form manifests. Knowing them, and seeing the world through the lens of *gunas* enables us to experience and describe things as their root origin, not as their secondary and infinite forms.

A candy bar, a double mocchiato, a new phone, a boxing match are all the energy of *rajas*. In these circumstances, there is only thing occurring. We respond to *rajas* in all of its infinite forms in exactly the same way. It provokes want, speed, and anxiety. It is the absolute reaction to movement energy.

A comfortable bed, obesity, lethargy, or even a mountain are all the energy of *tamas*. Here as well, there is only one thing occurring. The shadows of *tamas* portray many forms, and we might describe them in infinite ways, but to the yogi – only one thing is happening. That is the absolute reaction to non-movement energy.

Fasting, meditating, memorizing, practicing, and ecstatic dancing are all examples that transcend movement and non-movement. They create awareness. They facilitate the light of observance. Using them, we are given the vantage point to look beyond that which is experienced, and instead we see the being that which experiences.

And using all three of the *gunam* as root vertices, we acquire a powerful way to describe the context of where we are, and what we are surrounded by. Why we are influenced, and what we run away from.

We could argue over any spiritual text until the planet has turned to dust, its inhabitants have long faded away, and the sun has inhaled Pluto – or we could simply point to its energetic origin. Which *gunam* followed Jesus on the Sermon on the Mount? Which *gunam* did the Buddha perceive beneath the fig tree? Which *gunam* did Krishna offer to Arjuna before the battle? Which *gunam* does the atheist find in a noodly appendage?

Answering these questions, we no longer need the commentary. We see how the root energy evolves into the senses, and the myriad of experiences we entertain. We learn the purpose. The rest is just details.

Text 2.19

विशेषाविशेषलिङ्गमात्रालिङ्गानि गुणपर्वाणि
viśeṣa-aviśeṣa-liṅga-mātra-aliṅgāni guṇaparvāṇi

viśeṣa	Particular, special
aviśeṣa	Unparticular, undefined
liṅga	Distinctive, symbol
mātra	Reproducible
aliṅgāni	Nondisctinctive, nonsymbolic
guṇa	Of the three influences
parvāṇi	Stages, levels

The quality or state of experience can be broken into four ways : specific, unspecific, symbolic, or beyond symbolism.

All experience can be understood by its specificity and its symbolism. To illustrate this, imagine two people in a room with nothing but a lamp. One has a broken heart. The other does not. The one who is well perceives the light as unspecific, and non-symbolic. To her, it is quite simply a light. To the other, they see their lost lover, and the light reflects their pain.

In this way, one object can mean two completely different experiences separated by how specific and symbolic the object of their attention is. This is the architecture of perception. But instead of just a lamp, it involves an infinite amount of objects; some real, some imagined, some memories. Some of them specific, and some of them blurred and general. Each one defined by how far it's fled from our origin.

Lets consider how these ingredients came to be. They originated from pure consciousness. At the very beginning, there was only awareness. An awareness without form, identity, senses, or even a material world. It was simply awareness.

But then that awareness fractures. It becomes many. That many varied perceptions slowly drift away from this eternal experience. They find contact with an array of tools. Tools such as the body or the ears or an identity. Little by little, that original awareness begins to hear, feel, see, touch, and even be an individual. Each separated awareness entertaining itself by exploring specificity and symbolism. Where once there was one undifferentiated awareness -- now you are sitting in a park, reading a book, distracted by an insect, thinking of home.

Returning to our helpless lover analogy, we now can see the path that lead them to such despair. A once pure consciousness slowly became distracted by its byproduct. The infinite seeds of the material world came to life. Our poor lover was tempted and tantalized by its myriad of dreams, victories, and great loss. Each one varying in its range of symbolism and specificity. It becomes quite tricky to remember, that no matter how separated, symbolic, or specific our awareness becomes – we're only always a breath away from that origin. The two people, including the lamp, are simply extensions of this ocean of awareness.

Text 2.20

द्रष्टा दृशिमात्रः शुद्धोऽपि प्रत्ययानुपश्यः
draṣṭā dr̥śimātraḥ śuddho-'pi pratyaya-anupaśyaḥ

draṣṭā	The seer
dr̥śi	The power of seeing
mātraḥ	Only
ṣuddha	Pure
api	Even, although
pratyaya	Ideas of images of the mind
anupaśyaḥ	Witnesses

The seer perceives perfectly pure even though she or he is appearing to see some specific cognitive notion.

Let us, for a moment, separate awareness into two parts; the seer and the seen. In this way, we can examine what exactly is this mysterious seer, and what or even why exactly is something seen.

Patanjali, in this sutra, describes the seer as pure awareness. An awareness that remains pure regardless of what is seen. Even though a particular thought or particular thing exists, the consciousness still invariably remains pure and untouched. No circumstance, not even our own death can affect it -- awareness persists untouched, and impartial to the world among us.

That same undivided awareness trickles through every living being and uses us as an extension of itself. Because of this, we are by extension the distributed body of something far greater than just what lives among our planet. We are this eternal consciousness. Our bodies come and go, but the awareness does not.

So what exactly then is being seen? *Purusha* is the ancient Sanskrit word used to describe the awareness from which all things manifest. It is within this *purusha* that the material world originates. Much in the same way, our mind is a formless vacuum of creativity, but by some fluke of nature, life somehow evolves from its chaos. Because all things originate from this formless *purusha*, the only thing we can see, touch, taste, smell, or hear are varied reflections of this *purusha*. There is nothing in our known universe that isn't awareness. These very letters themselves are made up of the same awareness that perceives them.

And since you, my dear reader, are also pure consciousness – observing such reflections of yourself -- we can safely suggest that you are essentially pure consciousness revealing itself to itself.

Text 2.21

तदथ एव दृश्यस्याअत्मा
tadartha eva dr̥śyasya-ātmā

tad	His/Hers [the seer]
artha	Purpose, goal
eva	Only
dr̥śyasya	The seen, the knowable
ātmā	True self, essential nature

The purpose of the known is only for the soul to see.

As much as we like to admit we've designed our higher taste of things, it is actually the result of thousands of lives before us that gave us the platform and willpower to have those tastes.

A higher taste is a work-in-progress. The very nature of becoming aware of this preference, allows us to reach even higher tastes. Whether it is a healthier diet, a better career, or higher wisdom – through exploring awareness, we are carving and fine-tuning this higher taste.

This leads us to the great why we see what we do when we do. It's this taste that manifests the life ahead of you. Every single detail, every sound, every word, we see, think, and breathe – is all part of a sacred path. A road drawn from the center of our soul to the most outer regions of our sensual needs. It's a path woven by tastes and a series of events. Each experience, even as mundane as closing a kitchen cabinet, is a perfectly arranged part and parcel to this path. The will of our heart, as we close that kitchen cabinet, decides which direction we go among this path. And wherever the marble falls, the world reflects that ripple in our awareness.

You could say we move the world beneath our feet just by choosing an intention. Change the mind, and the places change. People change. And life will reflect. Even though we might be seeing the same people, witness the same events, we are as individuals, reading and manifesting something between the lines that's much deeper than the phenomenon of life itself.

The purpose of what we see is only for the soul to see. When we pursue a higher taste of awareness, every one of our waking dreams becomes a calling card to return to an even higher awareness. Each affirmation broadening the context, and leading us along the path.

This path should read like a book written by pure awareness. The words dissolve the reader. Every day, the page turns.

Text 2.22

कृतार्थं प्रतिनष्टंअप्यनष्टं तदन्य साधारणत्वात्
kr̥tārthaṁ pratinaṣṭaṁ-apy-anaṣṭaṁ tadanya
sādhāraṇatvāt

kr̥ta	Completed, accomplished
arthaṁ	Goal, purpose
prati	Toward, for
naṣṭam	Destroyed
apy	Although
anaṣṭaṁ	Not destroyed
tat	That
anya	Other [puruṣas]
sādhāranatvāt	Because of being universal

For the one whose purpose is accomplished, all objects cease to exist. However, for others, those objects still exist.

Existence isn't an individual experience. Neither is enlightenment. So long as just one person holds on to the form of non-reality, it will still exist. Take fear for example. As we draw ourselves inward in our meditation, we come to terms with our fear and settle it. Before long our fear is extinguished. But that doesn't mean that fear is extinguished throughout the world. This is because consciousness is both something we master on an individual level, and something we are obligated to share on a communal level among all living beings. This is one of the reasons why mindfulness leads to vegetarianism. Because the evolution of our individual awareness is absolutely relevant to the welfare of the life around us.

Text 2.23

स्वस्वामिशक्त्योः स्वरूपोप्लब्धिहेतुः संयोगः
svasvāmi-śaktyoḥ svarūp-oplabdhi-hetuḥ saṁyogaḥ

svasvāmi	The master's true self
śaktyoḥ	[The master's] changeable
svarūpa	self, power
upalabdhi	Nature, true form
hetuḥ	To understand
saṁyogaḥ	The cause
	Unity

The purpose of understanding the difference between our eternal nature and our changing characteristics is to find a perfect unity.

Our unity with life depends on knowing the difference between that which is eternal, and that which is destined to change. What is real, and what is not as real? It's a very difficult question to answer. The best way to observe anything is context. If you have the best context, then you have the best opportunity to know the difference. We could sit here all day and divvy up a myriad of qualities we think belongs to something eternal, or something superfluous — or we can just develop a sense of greater context and accomplish both goals simultaneously.

You will find that it doesn't matter whether you're staring at the feet of your greatest teacher, or the line to the bathroom. In the light of the greatest context, all things demonstrate superficiality and pure eternal nature. In the right context, any object can lead you in either direction. Knowing the difference between the two is the aftermath to the real work which is elevating the context.

Text 2.24

तस्य हेतुरविद्या
tasya hetur-avidyā

tasya	Of this [unity]
hetuḥ	The cause
avidyā	Ignorance

Identity comes from ignorance.

What we are is not who we are. Our name, our lifestyle, our body are all very secondhand details. These superfluous details came about after a very long chain events, some lasting for thousands of years. And in that fantastic series of events, we had all sorts of names, practiced a myriad of lifestyles, and carried a universe of different bodies. The constant that pierced through each of these experiences was an eternal awareness. An awareness that traversed from body to body into the body you currently foster. And this awareness will continue on indefinitely. It will inherit new names, new identities, and new bodies for an eternity.

To assume this short-lived body or this short-lived name, or even worse to assume these short-lived emotions or short-lived problems are who we are – we are completely missing the point. If rain fell on you, would you assume you're now the rain? When you use a computer, have you become the computer? In the same way, pure awareness uses the human body. Its infinite breadth passes through us and processes the world through our eyes, ears, nose, our touch, our heart, and creativity. And even though this body comes alive in its presence, it would be impractical to believe that we are this individual. We are still such an eternal awareness.

As such, we should not confuse this life of identification as our true self. We are so much more.

Text 2.25

तदभावात्संयोगाभावो हानं तद्दृशेः कैवल्यम्
tad-abhābāt-saṁyoga-abhāvo hānaṁ taddr̥śeḥ kaivalyam

tad	Whose
abhāva	To overcome, to remove
saṁyoga	Unity
hāna	Freedom, relinquish
tat	That
dr̥śeḥ	Of the seer
kaivalyam	Liberation

When false understanding ceases to exist between the seer and seen, when that union is completely abandoned, the force of seeing becomes liberated.

Letting the world be involves letting the world define itself outside of our lexicon. Meaning, the world just is. And there will never be a moment when we can truly identify what exactly it is or was or will be. It doesn't mean we have to abandon a practical language to interact with our lives, but we should always know that no matter how definitive our truths are, or how specific our inferences, we will never be able to succeed in actually describing something. Once we can let go of our need to know, then we can actually know. Then we can actually see.

Text 2.26

विवेकख्यातिरविप्लवा हानोपायः
viveka-khyātir-aviplavā hānopāyaḥ

viveka	Discrimination
khyātiḥ	Insight, discernment
aviplava	Uninterrupted
hanopāyaḥ	Means to an end

The means of removing illusioned perception is uninterrupted discriminative cognition.

We carry two seemingly identical forces. One is our truth and our limitless intention to love. The other is a series of coincidences. Success, money, a fantastic encounter, a new car, a great paying job -- is all coincidence. Both play out in our day to day, but very few of us can tell the difference. Knowing the difference is the first step. Our headlight among the fod is when that knowledge is uninterrupted.

Discriminating between love and coincidence, truth and materialism, is an act that is performed from all levels of the spiritual body; emotional and intellectual. It begins at a place before logic, before emotion, even before instincts. We call the world out. Are you real? What part of this serves my soul, and which part serves my fleeting illusions?

Yoga asana, japa, and meditation were very specifically designed to develop our discrimination. Breath after breath, we carefully simulate the phenomenon of life and choose the eternal over the material. We develop a taste for the transcendental. We develop a skill in differentiating between a truly natural reaction and the ego's reaction.

Text 2.27

तस्य सप्तधा प्रान्तभूमिः प्रज्ञ
tasya saptadhā prānta-bhūmiḥ prajña

tasya	His [the yogis']
saptadhā	Seven-fold
prānta-bhūmiḥ	Final stage
prajñā	Wisdom

One who has this discriminative knowledge will have seven types of ultimate insight.

We don't actually know the seven-fold path that Patanjali was referring to here. Scholars believe it must have been so popular at the time that there was no reason to describe it. But it also tells us two other important details. The first is that Patanjali was not the origin of the practice. The second is that because of this great gap in knowledge, Patanjali must have intended the Yoga Sutras to be accompanied by an authorized teacher.

So what are the seven? The *Mahābhārata* refers to seven *dhāranās*. The *Sānkya Kārikā* has seven *prānta-bhūmis*. I personally prefer Vyāsa's list of seven as he was one of the first commentators to the Yoga Sutras.

Therefore, I will include his as he was the closest authority to the original text. Without further ado, Vyasa's saptadhā.

1. The avoidable has been fully understood.
2. The causes of the avoidable have been destroyed.
3. The avoidance has been seen by the help of spiritual absorption.
4. An intellectual discernment has developed as a result.

5. The intellect finishes its duties.
6. The energies returns to their own cause.
7. The energies are no longer produced as there is no longer a necessity.

The first four are the only things we can personally do. Recognize suffering. End attachment. Look within. We don't even have to wait until we find something. We can immediately perform the fourth. Which is to allow the medium of this inward dialogue to exclusively be the way we express ourselves outwardly.

When this is practiced, the final three occur without us on their own time. The intellect will withdraw. It will no longer be needed. All the emotion, creativity, and fear that composed your personality will return to their formless origin. And since no one is no longer calling them, they will no longer return.

What is left is the hollow body of a living being. A being moved by pure awareness rather than a myriad of random coincidence. Or as Patanjali insists, one who will be able to discern.

Text 2.28

योगाङ्गानुष्ठानादशुद्धिक्षये ज्ञानदीप्तिराविवेकख्यातेः
yoga-aṅga-anuṣṭhānād-aśuddhi-kṣaye jñāna-dīptir-āviveka-khyāteḥ

yoga	Origin, union
āṅga	Limb
anuṣṭhānād	From the practice of
aśuddhi	Impurity
kṣaye	On the destruction of
jñāna	Knowledge, wisdom
dīptiḥ	To illuminate
ā	Up to, limitless
viveka	Discernment
khyāteh	Knowledge

Maintaining a daily practice of the rungs of yoga will destroy impurities, create wisdom and light and lead to discriminative knowledge.

The process of walking depends on the welfare of your feet, legs, stamina, and strength. The welfare of paying the rent depends on the welfare of your income, your financial planning, and choice of where to live. In yoga, the welfare of our conscious awakening is separated into eight interdependent parts. The more you understand these eight parts, the more you will understand the architecture of enlightenment. You will learn how this architecture relates to your lifestyle, what parts are strong or weak, and where we should go next. These eight steps are blueprints that have been hammered down, written and rewritten, by thousands of generations of yogis who have sacreficed their lives to consolidating and perfecting the means of the emancipated consciousness.

Text 2.29

यम नियमाअसन प्राणायाम प्रत्याहार धारणा ध्यान समाधयोऽष्टावङ्गानि
yama niyama-āsana prāṇāyāma pratyāhāra dhāraṇā
dhyāna samādhayo-'ṣṭāvaṅgāni

yama	Respect for others
niyama	Respect for yourself
āsana	Posture
prāṇāyāma	Breath control, energy
pratyāhāra	Withdrawel of the senses
dhāraṇā	Concentration
dhyāna	Meditation
samādhayaḥ	Absorption, enlightenment
aṣṭa	Eight
aṅgāni	Limbs

The eight limbs of yoga are code of self-regulations, the observances, energetic control, knowing the root of the senses, concentration, meditation, and perfected consciousness.

Each limb should be thought of codependently. Regardless of whether they are last or first, each contributes to the other's welfare equally. All eight of them illuminate the path towards liberation, and at the same time, liberation leads to the eight limbs. For example, practicing nonviolence will lead us to self-awareness. But just as well, self-awareness will lead us to nonviolence. So it's important to note that these eight limbs don't have to be even taught. They are our true nature. They will express themselves naturally when we are no longer puppeteered by our patterns. Vice versa, we can emulate them in order to discover ourselves.

The first six listed are things you do; abstinence, observance, energetic balance, withdrawel, and concentration. These are all things we practice within the yoga practice, individually or together, on and off the mat, doing everything we can to design a life a based on these principles.

The last two, meditation and perfected consciousness are things that happen to us. We can not practice these. We can only make available the time and place for them to occur by practicing the other six.

Nonetheless, it is just as important that they do occur as much as the other six. In order to ensure their appearance, we must renounce the fruits of our effort. Once we surrender all benefits of the practice, once we give up any future we might have with the practice, only then is there space for meditation to begin, and its result, perfected consciousness.

Text 2.30

अहिंसासत्यास्तेय ब्रह्मचर्यापरिग्रहाः यमाः
ahiṁsā-satya-asteya brahmacarya-aparigrahāḥ yamāḥ

ahiṁsā	Nonviolence
satya	Truthfulness
asteya	Non-stealing
brahma	God, a higher ideal
carya	Change towards
brahmacarya	Change towards a higher
aparigrahāḥ	ideal
yamāḥ	Non-covetousness
	Code of conduct

The code of self-restraint for the yogi is nonviolence, truthfulness, non-theft, kindred love, and non-posessiveness.

In order to understand the *yamāḥs*, you first must understand that there is no distance between this so called self and this so called world. What we are, the world is. What the world is, we are. Therefore, in order to develop this self, we must develop the world. In order to develop this world, we must develop the self. In this way, there is no I. It doesn't make any sense to say, I am being truthful. Or I am not being truthful. The *I* in these sentences is your spiritual materialism and ego distracting you.

Instead, if we surrender entirely to presence, and observe the soul that rests before the ego, you will find that you are by nature -- nonviolent, truthful, not-stealing, not-needing, and that you are the love you seek.

These *yamāḥs* essentially describe the effect of being present. But if we adhere to them, we enable ourselves to become present. In this way, they draw a material line we can see and experience. And this line helps us understand how present we actually are.

Text 2.31

जातिदेशकालसमयानवच्छिन्नाः सार्वभौमामहाव्रतम्

jāti-deśa-kāla-samaya-anavacchinnāḥ sārvabhaumā-mahāvratam

jāti	Birth, caste, social class
deśa	Location, place
kāla	Time
samaya	Circumstance, situation
anavacchinnāḥ	Limitless, unconditioned
sārva	In all, every
bhaumāḥ	Levels, place on Earth
mahā	Great
vratam	Vow

We take these yamas as a great vow to perform them universally, in all types of birth, anywhere, at anytime, in any circumstance.

The greatest gift in life is our attention. Our attention alone is the nectar that the world feeds from. Where ever your eyes or ears may rest, life will flourish. Where ever your will to listen resides, that's where your heart will unfold.

So we carefully maintain this fountainhead of our attention. It is a very sacred place from which our focus manifests. The *yamāḥs* were written to help us with this maintenance. If the *yamāḥs* are flawlessly maintained, then our awareness will come to us effortlessly. Likewise, if our awareness is flawlessly maintained, then the *yamāḥs* will come to us effortlessly.

What works against us is the human form. It's a very fickle body. We are very easily distracted. At every given moment our attention slips away. Yet, we know there's something more than just fickleness. We've experienced at varying degrees an awareness that is worth more than gold. And the *yamāḥs* is our vow to stay connected with that presence. They become a gateway between what is eternally true and what is temporarily us.

This sutra specifically reminds us that awareness is available to all life. Every being is conscious. Every flower, every mountain, every cloud is an extension of that awareness. In some cases, such as within a living being, they emulate that awareness through their eyes, or ears, or noses. Every specie has developed their own way to mirror that original eternal consciousness. Therefore, this vow of the *yamāḥs* will always be available to us. No matter what life we take birth in, we will always be able to maintain this vow.

And so because awareness transcends time and space, because it transcends circumstance -- we can always find a way to connect. Through birth after birth, we can carry with us our vow to become aware.

Text 2.32

शौच संतोष तपः स्वाध्यायेश्वरप्रणिधानानि नियमाः

śauca saṁtoṣa tapaḥ svādhyāy-eśvarapraṇidhānāni niyamāḥ

śauca	Cleanliness
saṁtoṣa	Contentment
tapaḥ	Austerity, sacrifice
svādhyāya	Self-study
īśvara	God, God-consciousness
praṇidhānāni	Devotion to
niyamāḥ	Observances towards self

The code of self-practice for the yogi is cleanliness, contentment, self-discipline, self-study and reflection, and pure surrender to God.

Where the *yamāḥ* is a description of our relationship with the world, the *niyamāḥ* is a description of our relationship with ourselves.

Just like the *yamāḥs*, these are a natural consequence of a higher consciousness. So by simply maintaining perfect *niyamāḥ*, higher consciousness will come effortlessly. Vice versa, if we are already enlightened, then the *niyamāḥs* come effortlessly. We would be by nature clean, content, self-disciplined, studying the self, and surrendering the fruits of our labor to something greater than just ourselves. No one would have to explain these features to such a person.

The *niyamāḥs* are a roadmap to the soul of every individual. They are a perfect description of each attribute we must acquire in order to fully perfect this living vehicle we call the self. Each one is intended as an action we can perfect until they individually become an aspect of our state of mind.

For example, cleanliness is an act. A clean home is a clean soul. A clean and healthy body is a restful mind. What begins in practice ends in awareness. When we practice contentment in the worst of situations, it's a simple practice that leads us to developing a mindset that's above cause and effect, triumph and failure. Sacrefice, self-study, and most of all devotion – are all things that begin as actions that end in awareness. Each *niyamāḥ* individually carves an integral part of our personality into its most wholesome origin. Each of these acts prepares us ultimately for the seemingly impossible act of meditation.

Text 2.33

वितर्कबाधने प्रतिप्रक्षभावनम्
vitarka-bādhane pratiprakṣa-bhāvanam

vitarka	Negative thoughts, doubt
bādhane	Enraptured by, harassing of
pratipakṣa	The opposite
bhāvanam	Cultivation

When deviant actions or thoughts inhibit the *yamāḥs* and the *niyamāḥs*, we follow them backwards to their origin.

Thoughts or actions will arrive that contradict our attention towards the yogic lifestyle. Patanjali teaches us how to transcend these contradictions by tracing their influence back to their origin. The key is simply questioning the origin of everything.

To question the origin of our desires and really listen to the response. Each question fashioning a trailhead back to their origin. An origin that reveals what triggers caused them. What experiences designed them. What fears and insecurities protect them.

Knowing that those triggers were never us is half the battle. We can end them. And we can end the direction that they would otherwise lead us. As we follow the footprints of every desire, allowing their origins to speak, we put each one to rest. One by one, allowing them to pass away in their own time. Each one losing its strength overtime. Until even their quiet whispering needs are just a memory.

We eventually consolidate the entire magnetic emotional body to its most natural and original state. It is from here, we respond to the world as it is. Rather than what we assume it is. The *yamāḥs* and *niyamāḥs* were designed to make us hyper aware of the details that distract our soul from being itself. We think of them as the rope the leads us through the labyrinth.

Text 2.34

वितर्का हिंसादयः कृतकारितानुमोदिता लोभक्रोधमोहाअपूर्वका
मृदुमध्य अधिमात्रा दुःखाज्ञानानन्तफला इति प्रतिप्रक्षभावनम्
vitarkā hiṁsādayaḥ kr̥ta-kārita-anumoditā lobha-krodha-moha-āpūrvakā
mr̥du-madhya adhimātrā duḥkha-ajñāna-ananta-phalā iti pratiprakṣa-bhāvanam

vitarkas	Doubt, negative thoughts
hiṁsādayaḥ	Violence
kr̥ta	Perpetrator
kārita	To instruct others to do
anumoditāḥ	The allower
lobha	Greed
krodha	Anger
moha	Illusion
pūrvaka	Preceded by
mr̥du	Mild
madhya	Moderate
adhimātrāḥ	Intense
duḥkha	Suffering
ajñāna	Ignorance
ananta	Never ending
phalāḥ	Resuls, outcome
iti	Thus
pratipakṣa	Opposite
bhāvanam	Cultivation

Deviations from the *yamāḥs* and *niyamāḥs* occur either by oneself, by others, or your approval. They are caused by desire, anger, and delusion, and travel in varying degrees thus spreading the cycle of suffering and ignorance. Thus so, the yogi relects on the root of these patterns.

Information spreads like a breeze. Any emotion be it anger, love, or uncertainty travels through us, through generations. The emotion manifests in our speech, in our work, sometimes carved into the buildings we surround ourselves with or the language we use. Just as a weatherman can predict the spread of humidity, one could also describe the spread of trauma across a land, its people, their culture, and the way the speak to each other.

A lot of the way we react to pain, or cause pain is apart of a much older, much greater movement that began thousands of years ago. Traces of past wars and ancient fears still affect and control the mannerisms of people who are completely removed from their origin.

The yogi knows this. They observe these patterns passing through the people and culture around them but is able to prevent these ancient emotional waves from affecting them by contemplating their origin.

Text 2.35

अहिंसाप्रतिष्ठायं तत्सन्निधौ वैरत्यागः
ahiṁsā-pratiṣṭhāyaṁ tat-sannidhau vairatyāghaḥ

ahiṁsā	Nonviolence
pratiṣṭha	Fixed
tat	Whose
sannidhau	In the presence
vaira	A state of feeling hostility
tyāghaḥ	Letting go

Nonviolence, once firmly established will end hostility.

Life is always trying to speak to you. Always trying to lead you, comfort you, offer you so many gifts. Nonviolence is the prerequisite to listening to this life. Nonviolence is also the prerequisite to being heard. The more nonviolent we are, the more we can communicate. The more life will communicate with us. We get to receive a better feedback for what we do. This feedback will guarantee us stability on our path. So if you're not interested in receiving feedback from the Earth you depend on, or the animals you survive off of -- then you have very little to learn, and no room to grow. Anyone can superimpose a fake world with fake walls that drown out the voice of the world around them. But the yogi's interest is to listen. It may not be necessary to go 100% eco-sustainable, or go vegan, or make some huge decision right now. But it's very important to start listening to every being you've made yourself codependent on. Listen to the animal before you slaughter them. Place your heart upon the Earth before you throw something away. Start with just a dialogue. See where it takes you.

Text 2.36

सत्यप्रतिष्थायं क्रियाफलाअश्रयत्वम्
satya-pratiṣthāyaṁ kriyā-phala-āśrayatvam

satya	Truthfulness
pratiṣṭham	Fixed
kriyā	Action
phala	Result
āśrayatvam	Being a foundation

Truthfulness, once firmly established, will result in the natural fruition of their actions.

If you consume truth, then your expression becomes truthful. But truth comes in many varying degrees. Truth isn't black and white. Pure truth is generally very difficult to recognize let alone to express.

There are so many variables that obscure our ability to see truth. Otherwise, we are lying. Just as we can very easily lie to ourselves about what feels good when it is actually terrible for us.

This is where a duty to our practice comes in handy. Because it's a duty that helps pierce through the dualism of, 'I don't want to do this', or 'I want to do this'. Instead, duty allows us to transcend the veil of our zig zagging emotions and say, "This is what it is". We discover something more permament and eternal once we can commit to something greater than our temporal day-to-day feelings. A duty to the practice allows us to sober our endlessly unsatisfied self to realism. And once the world gets real, we broaden the context of life to include the world around us not just us. Our expectations become realistic. Our perception becomes realistic.

Once we become truth, we see truth. Once we see truth, we become truth.

Text 2.37

अस्तेयप्रतिष्ठायां सर्वरत्नोपस्थानम्
asteya-pratiṣṭhāyāṁ sarvaratn-opasthānam

asteya	Not stealing
pratiṣṭhāyām	Fixed
sarva	All, everything
ratna	Jewels
upasthānam	Come near, be available

Non-stealing, once firmly established will make available all treasures.

In truth, nothing is ever yours. We can only move things around and to our best ability, and make it seem like they're 'more' ours. What the thief doesn't realize is that everything is always available to us. Our happiness, our peace, our love; it's all there waiting. And once the thief can abandon this play of 'this is more mine', they will realize that they can have the whole world. So don't let anything steal your breath. Instead, own the breath, and you will share the world.

Text 2.38

ब्रह्मचर्य प्रतिष्ठायां वीर्यलाभः

brahma-carya pratiṣṭhāyāṁ vīrya-lābhaḥ

brahmacarya	Transitioning towards the absolute
pratiṣṭhāyām	Fixed
vīrya	Power, potency
lābhaḥ	Gain, achieve

Brahmacarya once firmly established will have you attain strength, vitality, and courage.

We can enjoy the diversity of flavor if we refrain from fast food. We can appreciate better the space between notes in music if the composition is not overcrowded. In all these cases, if a material object monopolizes our magnetism, then we will never notice the other things our spirit craves.

Lust, unlike hunger or greed, can be one of the most pervasive of all attractions. It can blend in with any other mundane action. Our interest in power, our social dynamism, even our choice in foods can all be sexually influenced. And as a result, if we don't understand the power of sexual energy, we can be very easily manipulated by sexual desire rather than our better interests.

The solution for many spiritual seekers is abstinence. Remove the sexual urge and desire becomes clarified. The purer the magnetism, the easier it is for us to navigate the subtler attractions we have. When the cravings diminish, we begin to see the strings that puppeteer them. Layer by layer removed, we can discover the architecture of this innate desire and what intention is directing us. When followed to its source, we are lead through several layers of motive; the avoidance of self, the urge to connect with others, or the will to procreate.

There's nothing inherently wrong with any of these intentions. Distracting our self from our self can be an incredible way to elevate the consciousness. Witnessing others in such intimate formation can be elevating. Giving birth and procreation can indescribable spiritual growth.

But the difference between conscious awareness and puppeteering is knowing who holds the strings and for what reasons they make us dance. There isn't a black and white answer. There are an infinite number of shades between knowing and actually knowing.

So I will leave you with this. Brahmacharya is in very basic terms, learning that you are the love you seek. Everything you're looking for outside of you is already within you; the absolute reality, God's love, it's all there. People who don't know how to find that selfless and sweet inner love will never be satisfied in this life. And sex is very often their prescribed choice of diversion.

But when the heart is full of love, and you discover that you are the love you seek, sexuality becomes superfluous. You can always trust your inward intentions. And from them, acquire strength, vitality, and courage.

Text 2.39

अपरिग्रहस्थैर्ये जन्मकथंता संबोधः
aparigraha-sthairye janma-kathaṁtā saṁbodhaḥ

aparigraha	Non-covetousness
sthairye	Steadfastness, steady
janma	Caste, class, birth
kathaṁtā	The howness
saṁbodhaḥ	Knowledge

Once you have found stability in non-attachment, you will understand how and from where all things originate.

Most of this world we will never know. But we are naturally unsatisfied with not knowing. So we start filling in what we don't know with clever assumptions that inadvertently make us know less, and crave more assumptions. More assumptions, more ignorance. More ignorance, more assumptions. Very soon, our entire life becomes a patchwork of plastic reality.

To practice *aparigraha*, or non-attachment , we welcome uncertainty. Question after question, we respond with the loving affection to let go and not know. When we don't need to know, we no longer assume. No assumptions, no ignorance. No ignorance, no bias. The world can be just as the world is. With no middleman in between the phenomon of life and our awareness, we can begin to see the truth in how all things originate.

A great practice of *aparigraha* is the Zen tradition of koans. These are questions that have us meditate in a space between an impossible question and an infinite answer. Master Sekiso gives one such example asking, "You are at the top of the 100 foot high pole. How will you make a step further?"

Text 2.40

शौचात् स्वाङ्गजुगुप्सा परैरसंसर्गः
śaucāt svāṅga-jugupsā parairasaṁsargaḥ

śaucāt	Cleanliness
svāṅga	One's own body
jugupsā	Distaste, distanced from
paraiḥ	With others
asaṁsargaḥ	Ending association

Cleanliness of the body and mind creates a distance between one's body and mind and the world.

An abandoned home among the forest will eventually crumble to nature. Nature will shatter its windows, crawl through its walls, and pull it back into the Earth it stood from. An abandoned home has no choice.

A consciousness, on the other hand, has a choice. It's because of this ability to choose, we understand that a state of mind can transcend its own entropy. Unlike the abandoned home, the consciousness can maintain itself away from collapse. It can define a distance between itself and the world that resonates from it.

The yogi in particular celebrates this distinction with cleanliness. Our cleanliness reflects the distance we maintain between awareness and the world we are aware of. Just as dirt and sweat and smell collects on the body, our awareness collects the phantasmagoria we witness. Our memories become objects on the bookshelves of our consciousness. In time, we begin to confuse our awareness for those objects. We mistake our memories for our presence. We mistake the the world for who we are.

Cleanliness distinguishes awareness from the body-mind machine our awareness uses. We might scrub the mind of false ego. Or wash our soul in mantra. Or bathe in a higher context. Or simply have a shower. In each case, we are revealing the consciousness that hides in the nature.

But the body has no borders. Therefore, cleanliness begins with our skin and water but it extends to the welfare of our rivers, forests, and skies. As a clean Earth also facilitates a spiritual distance between awareness and the world born from awareness. The seeker sees no finite end to this sense of expression.

Text 2.41

सत्त्वशुद्धिः सौमनस्यैकाग्र्येन्द्रियजयाअत्मदर्शन योग्यत्वानि च
sattva-śuddhiḥ saumanasya-ikāgry-endriyajaya-
ātmadarśana yogyatvāni ca

sattva	Truth
śuddhiḥ	Purification
saumanasya	Cheerfulness
ekāgrya	Single pointed focus
indriya	Senses
jayā	Mastery, control
ātma	The soul
darśana	Direct seeing
ātmadarśana	Realization of the soul
yogyatvāni	Qualification
ca	And, also

Cleanliness also leads to the purification of your true identity, clarity, one-pointedness, control over the cognitive senses, and the physical ability of experiencing the source of consciousness.

Cleanliness is the prerequisite to defining the body as a vehicle of transcendence and not of reaction. To understand this, imagine threads of emotional history crawling through time. Threads not unlike the dirt we acquire by walking barefoot. These threads are composed of trauma and are passed through the hands of generations of people who further their passage by reacting and not acting. They make up the vernacular of how we communicate, our culture, and values. The reason these threads survive is because the individuals the trauma passes through are of people who don't know themselves, nor know how they're being affected by such inertia. You could say, their awareness is not clean. And the dirtier it gets, the more dirt it acquires.

Cleanliness is an art form and a means of posturing ourselves away from mindless reaction. It is the absolute reset. And when you reset, you're offered the scope of your true identity, and the ability to perceive a larger context in life. We cleanse our material body with water. But we can only truly cleanse our self with meditation and mantra. This eases the years, if not generations, of karma we accumulated. Layer by layer, we come to see the being inside of us who is karma-less. That is, a being unafilliated with what they experience. A being who is completely pure.

Text 2.42

संतोषातनुत्तमस्सुखलाभः
saṁtoṣāt-anuttamas-sukhalābhaḥ

saṁtoṣāt	Contentment
anuttamaḥ	The highest
sukha	Joy
lābhaḥ	Attained

From contentment, supreme joy is attained.

Your bliss is always available to you. Always. We don't allow ourselves to be happy because we have convinced ourselves that happiness has to be earned and paid for by certain circumstances. Only once those circumstances occur, do we feel justified to even allow ourselves to feel contentment.

This obstacle to our joy originates from having suffered abuse. Because abuse of any kind tells us that we don't deserve our happiness. And so long as we can't let go of our pain, we have to juggle having our joy only if our pain allows it. So if you don't feel comfortable with being at peace right now without reason, then first start by letting go of all the suffering you're still clinging to. In simpler words, be content.

Remind yourself, you are not your pain. You don't owe your pain anything. Happiness doesn't have to be earned, it's simply realized. You have the right to be happy because it's your nature to do so.

Text 2.43

कायेन्द्रियसिद्धिरशुद्धिक्षयात् तपसः
kāyendriya-siddhir-aśuddhi-kṣayāt tapasaḥ

kāya	The body
indriya	Senses
siddhiḥ	Powers, perfections
aśuddhi	Impurities
kṣayāt	From the removal
tapaḥ	Self-discipline, sacrifice

By removing impurities via selfless dedication, the body and its senses are perfected.

We can only progress in our practice when we have renounced the fruit of our efforts. Meaning, progress doesn't physically or emotionally begin until we stop yearning for a goal. The practice itself is the ends. Flexibility, strength and emotional resoluteness is the side effect – but it is commonly mistaken as a goal.

Until we find ourselves in a mundane pose, between a mundane breath count, and say, here I am as I am, we're only going to develop a mindset of constant dissatisfaction. Always underwhelmed by our breath. Always underwhelmed by our effort and our practice.

This generally aggravates the beginner, and most of the time turns them away from the practice entirely. And ironically as a result of this dispassion, they never get flexible, strong, or feel spiritually complete.

So really, the only skill one needs to learn from yoga is selfless service. Hold on to this and all will follow. The body and the senses and heart will follow. You'll soon discover that selfless service is in and of itself the perfection of yoga.

Text 2.44

वाध्यायादिष्टदेवता संप्रयोगः
svādhyāyād-iṣṭa-devatā saṁprayogaḥ

svādhyāyat	Learning from the self
iṣṭa	Desired, loved
devatā	God-consciousness, ideal
saṁprayogaḥ	Union

From the study of God we become connected to God.

The word *God* can accomplish what other words can't. Unlike most of our language, the word *God* is a transcendental word. It points to something beyond material awareness. And it's so good at being transcendental that any given person would describe it differently, almost poetically if they were asked. This is because there's no perfect answer.

But that doesn't negate that there's an experience that can be shared in presence. And by dwelling in any word that represents God, be it Hashem, Jesus, Allah, Krishna, Govinda – we are also dwelling in a transcendental state of mind. The words lead to a context.

Transcendental words like *God* work the exact same way as higher math does. Having access to more complicated numbers gives a greater context of greater equations. Infinities are beautiful example of this. Such as Fibonacci's sequence or Pi travel indefinitely, almost eternally. They exist with or without us being aware of them. Dwelling in them leads us to an infinite mindset. One that humbles us to the awareness that some things are far greater than our ability to understand.

But these are just the words. Nothing more. The words should be seen as the residue of an experience, but not the experience itself. Words like God, or Pi, or Krishna are just the placeholder for an infinite well of experience. But it's that placeholder that allows us to investigate their origin. And if we reflect on these words, we can follow the trail they leave behind. Back to the experience that gave birth to them. *Svādhyāyat* is the practice of following these trails.

Text 2.45

समाधि सिद्धिःईश्वरप्रणिधानात्
samādhi siddhiḥ-īśvarapraṇidhānāt

samādhi	Enlightened state
siddhiḥ	Power, attainment
īśvara	God, God-consciousness
praṇidhāna	Devotion towards, surrender

By mastering total surrender to something greater than yourself, enlightenment is attained.

The reason pollution, war, or racism exists at all is because most people refuse to acknowledge a world outside of themselves. No one is exempt from being responsible for these things. To some varying degree, we have all taken part in destroying one another and the world around us by not trying to perceive something greater than just us.

Enlightenment is based on how broad of a context you can see outside of the self. The smallest context are those who imagine themselves as the center of the universe. Others may have found love and their context exists in the welfare of a few people outside of themselves.

The yogi, however, attempts at broadening their context infinitely. The actual broadening of this context is achieved through love as devotion is the act of serving something outside of ourselves. By serving something beyond our interests, we broaden our perception.

Love allows us to see things like pollution, war, pain, or any of our mistakes before they occur. Because suddenly, we can see the world our actions take place within, and not just how our actions serve ourselves.

To achieve this great context, we serve unconditionally the greatest object. In Vedic philosophy we refer to this as *ishvara*, our spiritual locus, our creative origin, or in Western vernacular, God. And by rendering our thoughts and actions as selfless gifts to this broader context, we can begin to see a world outside of ourselves, our generation, our species, and even our universe. Otherwise, the ego sees nothing until it surrenders the palace it hides within.

Text 2.46

समाधि सिद्धिःईश्वरप्रणिधानात्

sthira-sukham-āsanam

sthira	Steady, stable
sukham	Joyful, comfortable
āsanam	Posture

Meditation begins with steady, comfortable pose.

The real power in asana is when we are challenged. Poses that force us to negotiate with layers of our emotional and intellectual fears and nuances. Through years of commitment to a particular sequence, or duration of asana – we arrive at a colorful dialogue of ourself. A picture painted by our strengths and weaknesses, attractions and doubts.

We come to learn the most intimate aspects of our instincts. We learn why we run. Why we fight. How we hate. We learn how fear and love string us like a marionette and dance us through life after life without us ever being aware.

Asana is by no means a goal. It is simply a preparation for meditation. In many ways, it is almost impossible to speak directly to our awareness. And so we use the body as a communiqué between the material world and the soul it represents. It's through our commitment to the body that inklings of this inner self begins to shine through.

The pose itself is the tip of the iceberg. But the nectar of the practice is found in the compromise we make to afford the time to practice. Or in the humility we use to navigate our injuries. The acceptance we hold as our body ages, grows tender, breaks down, and passes on. In this way, our intellect and our soul can share a dialogue through a short-lived being.

Text 2.47

प्रयत्नशैथिल्यानन्तसमापत्तिभ्याम्

prayatna-śaithilya-ananta-samāpatti-bhyām

prayatna	Effort
śaithilya	Relaxation
ananta	Without ending
samāpatti	Absorption of the infinite
abhyām	Both

Any pose delivers us to infinite absorption when it is composed of both tension and release.

Our awareness is like a sun passing over the body. It rises and touches every nerve ending with direction. In every subtle aspect of us, it nurtures a dance of tension and release. And then it sets and surrenders us to autopilot.

The magic of this awareness is in its tension and release. These two elements are the designers of life. They manifest the ocean's tides, compose music, and design the human vertebrae. You could say that tension and release are the only tools required to recreate the universe.

And we discover these tools by practicing them with the body. It's far easier to explain the body than the depths of our consciousness. And so yoga *āsanam* offers us a simple means of interacting with an impossible awareness. And what we learn from this physical nature translates to the emotional and transcendental natures. What we practice internally gets projected externally and eventually survives us.

And so in the physical practices we reenact this ancient mechanism of tension and surrender, creation and destruction, *rajas* and *tamas*. By the same means the world was formed, we scan the whole of the body-mind architecture with them. We teach ourselves their fundamentals in every bodily system, nerve ending, and sensory organ. Whether it's the breath, the pose, the pumping of the heart, or the drive of an intention, all movement is somewhere between the duality of tension and release.

Whether our aspiration is the wellbeing of the universe, or the peace in our friends and family – the practice begins within, and the process is tension and release.

Text 2.48

ततो द्वङ्द्वानभिघातः
tato dvaṅdva-an-abhighātaḥ

tataḥ	From that [āsanam]
dvaṅdva	By those dualities
anabhighātaḥ	Free from affliction

Through that tension and release, duality loses its effect.

Tension and release may compose sound, but they do not describe the quality of music. This is because tension and release administer the material effect of sound, but the soul is the judge of music. So we should see this duality of tension and release as the penultimate duality and the key to disillusioning ourselves from their effect.

In yoga *āsanam*, tension and release is reenacted in posture, breath, *bandha, drsti,* and intention. Together, they challenge us to the brink of our emotional and physical capacity. We become intimate with the effect of a little extra tension or a little more surrender. We're pushed to the extreme subtle edge of consciousness. Observing these ever so slight consequences on our awareness, we see how these same forces manipulate and design the world around us.

Practicing this day after day, year after year, we become a little less interested in the perfection and loss of sound. And instead, we acquire a taste for essence of music. Just as a *sadhu* day after day, year after year becomes a little less interested in having a job, a marriage, children, and wealth. Instead the *sadhu* acquires a taste for higher love. And from that love, duality in all its expansive variations of success and loss, war and peace, tension and release – became secondhand and unnecessary.

Text 2.49

तस्मिन् सति श्वासप्रश्वास्योर्गतिविच्छेदः प्राणायामः
tasmin sati śvāsa-praśvāsyor-gati-vicchedaḥ prāṇāyāmaḥ

tasmin	After that [āsanam]
sati	Attained
śvāsa	Inhaling
praśvāsyoḥ	Exhaling
gati	Movement
vicchedaḥ	Regulating, interrupting
prāṇa	Life force, energy
āyāma	Release, liberate
prāṇāyāmaḥ	Liberation of life force

Upon finding our āsana, we accomplish it by slowing and softening the unregulated breath through the inhalation and exhalation. This is called pranayamah, or the regulation of prana, our energetic connection between breath and consciousness.

The emotional reality of the world around us is reflected in the breath. It describes an emotional landscape through its stutter, its pause, and every other nuance of an inhalation and exhalation.

Every single one of our body's chemical reactions, our eleven body systems, and blood pressure are regulated via the breath alone. Beings both past and current have been able to sustain prolonged exposure to extreme cold, heat, trauma, depth, and physical endurance simply by mastering this single apparatus. It is without a doubt, easy to suggest that the mastered breath also leads to altered state of expansive awareness, intellect, and imagination.

Once we see that the awareness and the mind-body machine are two distinct entities, we realize that the style of breath is the means by which awareness puppeteers the machine. Augment the breath and you tweak the body's movements and the phantasmagoria of the consciousness.

Text 2.50

बाह्याअभ्यन्तरस्थम्भ वृत्तिः देशकालसन्ख्याभिः परिदृष्टो दीर्घसूक्ष्मः
bāhya-ābhyantara-sthambha vr̥ttiḥ deśa-kāla-sankhyābhiḥ paridr̥ṣṭo dīrgha-sūkṣmaḥ

bāhya	External
abhyantara	Internal
stambha	Restrained, suspension
vr̥ttiḥ	Thought wave
deśa	Place
kāla	Time
saṁkhyābhiḥ	Number
paridr̥ṣṭo	Verified, manifested
dīrgha	Long
sūkṣmaḥ	Subtle

The architecture of breath is composed of three components; inhalation, exhalation, and retention. Which are then augmented by location, duration, and count. They are observed by extending their subtle qualities.

In just one cycle of the breath, your entire life can be read to you. You can hear how many times your heart has been broken. How many times you've cried in joy. Every detail about you is saved in the fingerprint of a breath. Vice versa, we can communicate to the very core of our essence and that of others by composing a breath specially designed to share our awareness and aspirations.

Just as each nuance of the breath leaves behind a clue to our past, we can shape those same nuances to design our presence. In a very obvious way, we begin this by simple taking a deeper breath. An act that alludes the majority of us in the stressful lives we live. Immediately this takes an effect on our emotional state and our capacity to retain information.

But deeper than this is when we explore techniques of breath retention and observe how closely intertwined the sympathetic nervous and endocrine systems are to our ability to relax under the duress of oxygen. With the breath alone, one could sustain hours of being submerged in glacier water or slow the heartbeat to an unperceivable rhythm.

In any of these practices the directions are very clear. There is a very particular way to draw, expel , or retain the air. Changing the pressure of the breath in various parts of the body, the duration, or count can completely alter the effect of the body and consciousness.

Just as we can elongate a sound wave to study its minutiae of detail, the same can be applied to *pranayama*. By extending and slowing the breathing practice, we can look into the gradual effect it has on the organ of awareness, our energy, and the body.

Text 2.51

बाह्याअभ्यन्तर विषयाक्षेपी चतुर्थः
bāhya-ābhyantara viṣaya-akṣepī caturthaḥ

bāhya	External
viṣayā	Internal
bāhya -ābhyantra	External retention
abhyantra-viṣayā	Retention after inhaling
ākṣepī	Surpassing
caturthaḥ	The fourth

The fourth component of pranayama exists beyond the realm of exhalation and inhalation, external and internal retention.

Deep behind the surface of our breathing apparatus is a hidden place. It is a secret place from which all energy emerges. On the surface of the breath, through retention, inhalation, and exhalation – we draw from this well.

This fourth pranayama is independent of the breath. It is inherent. Yet our breathwork and retention techniques reflect this deeper energy. And they eventually lead us to this body.

Just as any body of moving water will lead us to an ocean. Our inhalations, exhalations, and retentions lead us like an elegant brook or a trailing river. Each of our breaths as unique as a particular brook or an elegant river. And just like the river, every given breath is leading us to and from an energetic origin, an ocean. Though we may never experience this ocean directly, we gather hints of its depth from the experiences we collect in pranayama.

And we inch closer to an awareness that transcends the rise and fall of our biological limits. Noticing the fourth pranayama, the origin of prana, is like a wildflower noticing a crack through the pavement.

Text 2.52

ततः क्षीयते प्रकाशाअवरणम्
tataḥ kṣīyate prakāśa-āvaraṇam

By that fourth pranayama, the veil that covers your inner light is destroyed.

tataḥ	Then
kṣīyate	Destroyed, weakened
prakāśa	Illumination
āvaranam	Covering

In most conflict, for the sake of survival, we are programmed to either fight or run away. This fight or flight response is passed on generation after generation, life after life, like a thread woven between millennium of cultures and language. Rarely do we have the physical or cognitive ability to express ourselves outside of this instinct for power. Even if we're established as a successful doctor, or a wealthy landowner; our success is likely just a coincidence of a highly intelligent being performing the same fight or flight instincts as that of a cat or a bird or a cockroach.

Philosophers as old as time insist humans are different from animals specifically because we have accomplished the written language, quantum theory, or telecommunications. But we could equally argue that these vices would have been accessible to any intelligent life form regardless of whether they were conscious or not. In short, awareness and intelligence should be understood as mutually exclusive. Science is a natural coincidence of survival. Enlightenment is not.

The object of the Yoga Sutras as a whole is to transcend this dualist thought. Instead of karma being bad versus good, we observe simply a cause and effect. Instead of energetic versus lazy, we learn to appreciate the movement of awareness. And instead of the breath being maintained by apparatus, retention, or technique, we study here that pranayama is a stateless energy that neither comes nor goes. It rests somewhere deeper than the breath. Breath control is just a window into this greater well within us.

The perfection of pranayama is discovering this well. The more we move from this stateless source, the more stateless we recognize the things around. When we can perceive a stateless world, then we are no longer driven by the inertia of fighting and running because there's no longer anything to fight or run from. There's no longer a power to consolidate. No longer a need to survive because even death itself is superfluous. This is when your inner light is revealed. When you can truly be you.

Text 2.53

धारणासु च योग्यता मनसः
dhāraṇāsu ca yogyatā manasaḥ

Once pranayama is mastered, then concentration becomes available as it depends on the physiological and cognitive processes of the mind.

dhāraṇāsu	For concentration
ca	And
yogyatāḥ	Fitness
manasaḥ	Mind

Affirmation is never enough. Hearing a guru say something brilliant is refreshing, but knowing alone isn't enough. Alan Watts was a celebrated academic of the consciousness, but he still died of alcoholism and was known for his womanizing. So just knowing these sutras, listening to great teachers has nothing to do with the foundation of your conscious awareness.

Your conscious awareness depends on a physiological process, trained through repetition and good health. It's the same with your ego, your addictions, your patterns good or bad -- they are all neurological patterns governed by the audience you give them.

Prabhupada taught his devotees to chant 16 to 64 japas a day, which could take close to eight hours to complete. His devotees learned how to cognitively master a sense of devotion. Their devotion became stronger than their animal instincts. And as a result, they gained access to their souls.

Text 2.54

स्वविषयासंप्रयोगे चित्तस्य स्वरूपानुकारैवेन्द्रियाणां प्रत्याहारः
svaviṣaya-asaṁprayoge cittasya svarūpānukāra-iv-
endriyāṇāṁ pratyāhāraḥ

sva	Their own
viṣaya	Sense object
asaṁprayoge	Not coming into contact
cittasya	with
svarūpa	Of the mind
anukāra	Our nature
eva	Imitation
indriyāṇām	Like
pratyāhāraḥ	Of the senses
	Withdrawel of the senses

Pratyahara is the withdrawl of sense cognition from our thought patterns.

Materialism is a casino where the house always wins. Our senses are the slot machines. Because of a few unlikely wins near the birth of our bodies, a desperate need arose and has haunted us ever since. We pay in presence what we only rarely gain in feeling fulfilled. And we become addicted to it.

People camp these casinos day after day waiting for a win. Their focus is hypnotized and they willfully hand over their life savings for something they can never achieve. But the casinos are not just cheap carpets, bright lights, and fake games. The greatest casino ever designed is the body you live within. Where every passing moment is a rigged game of the senses. We gamble for short-lived experiences, and we pay for it with our identity. The more we lose the less we are.

Only for brief and sudden moments does it seem like we're ahead. Perhaps a long-term goal was achieved. Perhaps the ice cream was sweet. But then we suddenly find ourselves empty and under valued once again.

The reason we gamble is for one very simple and crucial reason. The gambler forgets that they are the love they seek. They seek elsewhere, and they seek for less. Their sense of taste cheapens. Their cognitive makeup and social life follow. You could offer them eternal bliss, and they'll ignore you for a chance at winning a weak smile.

Pratyahara is stepping away from the game. Taking a step away from the senses. Until the only thing left is what comes from within. And that, my friend, is the very beginning to actually winning.

Text 2.55

ततः परमावश्यता इन्द्रियाणाम्
tataḥ paramā-vaśyatā indriyāṇām

tataḥ	From this
paramā	Highest
vaśya	Mastery, control
indriyāṇām	Of the senses

Therefore by practicing pratyahara, you will have perfected the highest mastery of cognition.

This mind-body machine is merely representing a grain of sand from a desert of experience. In order to perceive the desert, we have to stop feeding the fever of our small mind needs. We only see as far as we're willing to let go of our sight. We only taste as much as we're willing to abandon our taste.

The mastery of sense gratification isn't finding the perfect experience, but perfecting the art of experiencing. Just as those who enjoy the most expect the least. The quality of the object is unnecessary. It's the welfare of our awareness that decides how sweet the ice cream is or how beautiful the river lays. Just as the sweetness of freedom can only be tasted by those who know prison.

Regardless of how committed we are, how frugal or ascetic, we only truly master the senses when the context of experience is greater than the experience itself. Such as when we admire the beauty of our soul through the allure or tragedy of this world. At this point, it's no longer a skill or a lifestyle choice. It is a context that transcends our time here on Earth.

Chapter Three

Text 3.1

देशबन्धः चित्तस्य धारणा
deśa-bandhaḥ cittasya dhāraṇā

deśa	Place
bandha	Bound
cittasya	Of the mind, consciousness
dhāraṇā	Concentration

Dhāraṇā is binding all thought to one place.

Just as we can say, we are what we eat – wherever our attention goes, so we will be. As such, we study various seats of focus. Each one varying the fountainhead of our imagination. Slightly augmenting our personality and direction. Whether it's the lotus feet of our teacher, the chameleon of presence, or the stale repetition of our unconscious habits – wherever our focus rests, that is what we become. That is what the world is.

It's because of this, we should observe our ability to focus as a powerful tool. It is, by itself, a mystic power very few animals share. We not only can focus on the things around us, but also the means in which we focus. And as we develop the means, we sustain the object. Whatever flavor of concentration we assume, it manifests not just the object of our focus but the environment that sustains it.

My favorite example is presence. It is an immeasurable locus. Always fleeting. To focus on presence means that we're focused on the context of our awareness. Not so much the object. By practicing this, we develop an environment of awareness more so than the remembrance of something in particular. And consequentially, the environment manifests a world that sustains itself. We suddenly find ourselves surrounded by people, places, and things that supplement and sustain that focus.

Another example are those that focus on the qualities of God. Be it one of God's beautiful physical descriptions or their consciousness. The means of focus is love and service. It's that focus that manifests an environment of love and service, and its that environment that manifests a world that sustains its intention.

In chapter two we introduced the eightfold path. Of which only five were mentioned. They illuminate a road leading from the most external of our habits such as nonviolence, non-stealing, and truthfulness – to a secret place within at the fountainhead of presence. It is here in the third chapter, we open a door to the last three rungs, that when combined, produce mystic powers. The first of which is concentration.

Text 3.2

तत्र प्रत्ययैकतानता ध्यानम्

tatra pratyaya-ikatānatā dhyānam

tatra	There, then
pratyaya	Idea, concept
eka	One
tāna	To flow, migrate
ekatānata	One continuous flow
dhyānam	Meditation

Dhyāna is single uninterrupted cognition over time.

Meditation is awareness in motion. Awareness isn't just cognizance of, let's say, an apple laying before you. It's awareness of that apple over time. And this is what differentiates the experience of an apple from every living being. Because after some time passes, the experience of perceiving an apple comes packaged with your random memories and distractions that are unique to just you.

So what you're really looking at, is not an apple at all. What you're looking at, is your reaction to staring at an apple. Your actually looking at yourself. The apple is just a temporary reference to how your consciousness operates.

Meditation is using the apple to study and understand how and why your imagination is designed, and where exactly all these wild thoughts come from. Focus on an object long enough, and you will see it. Focus on it even longer, and you will see yourself.

Text 3.3
तदेवार्थमात्रनिर्भासं स्वरूपशून्यमिवसमाधिः
tadeva-artha-mātra-nirbhāsaṁ svarūpa-śūnyam-iva-samādhiḥ

tad	That, hence
eva	The same, actually
artha	Object
mātra	Alone, only
nirbhāsā	Luminous, shining forth
svarūpa	Own nature
śūnyam	Empty, devoid of
iva	As if, like
samādhiḥ	State of enlightenment

Samādhi is losing the self completely, existing only within a point of focus.

In the past few hundred years, we've had the special privilege of growing up in our own rooms. We can lock the doors. We can collect all sorts of relics. We can decorate the walls. We choose color schemes, accents, and even the smell. It becomes a novelty echo chamber. We call this a home.

But it's also called an ego. Insulated by isolation. Handcrafted by what serves our cry for power and pleasure. And very recently, easily converted into a consumer product via television, lifestyle magazines, and Instagram. Now, not only can we mentally separate ourselves from others, but we can charge for it as well.

Not before long, we become an island to ourselves. Should anything in this world ask us to evolve, there will be someone or something reassuring you that it's unnecessary. Should you become addicted to drugs or should the environment become emaciated, someone or something will always be there to remind you that it's your own little island, and you're its king.

But there's a door outside this cushioned home. It's a door called surrender. It has a powerful way of tearing down walls. It can be done by devotion. Some surrender by just awareness. Whatever way you surrender, the implication is that we're accepting something outside. Something beyond our plush lifestyle and comfy affirmations. There's even rumor of life like us.

Much in the same way someone might grow disinterested in the hyperrealistic facades of an amusement park to instead find more sincerity in a cup of tea with one of its employees. What leads us to the amusement is our need for distracting pleasure. What leads us beyond the amusement is our will for reality.

Samādhi is both the result and the origin of yoga. When we focus on something long enough, we become it. We see ourselves through it. But the self we see isn't who was looking. It's something just beyond our material perception. The only thing in the way is you.

Text 3.4

त्रयमेकत्र संयमः
trayam-ekatra saṁyamaḥ

trayam	The three
eka	One
ekatra	Together
saṁyamaḥ	Absorption, meditation

Saṁyama is when dhāraṇā, dhyāna, and samādhi are performed together.

Saṁyama is the hand that designs enlightenment. It is the primary tool of the yogi. Each of its separate parts lead the practitioner from their intention to what is the origin of life. It's a process that describes the abdication of the self. Beginning with what is our will to expand our awareness. Then it ultimately ends in our awareness merging with the world outside of ourselves.

The technique blurs borders. It blurs the border between the individual and the universe. It diminishes the distance between the logical and the impossible. Whether its levitation, immortality, or unfathomable strength, the gateway to these mystic powers is composed from combining the last three rungs of the eightfold path; focus, meditation, and *samādhi.*

Beginning with *dhāraṇā*, focus – this is the only actual choice we make among these three rungs. The rest are up to the world. But our attention is ours to make. We choose a locus, and the world suspends around it. Depending on where it rests, the world unfolds.

Meditation or *dhyāna*, depends on the welfare of our environment to sustain this focus. You could say, it's the environment that is practicing, and you are simply a part of it. In this way, you the individual are exerting no effort. The world isn't chasing you towards or away from a practice. It's just happening.

And should we meditate sufficiently, the third stage begins. The very essence of our being is revealed to the very essence of our focus. In some traditions, this is the total loss of self, object, and acting of perception. A state of oneness. In other traditions, this is described as the purest medium of love. Where even when presented with the ability to merge into oneness, we deny it for the opportunity to serve such a love. This is called *samādhi* or total absorption.

Whichever *samādhi* one uncovers, they all ultimately lead to the same place. But the journey, especially the paths just before this experience, comes rife with mystic powers and impossible challenges. For better or worse, what we perceive, we become.

Text 3.5

तज्जयात् प्रज्ञालोकः
tajjayāt prajñālokaḥ

tat	That, there
jayāt	From mastery
prajñā	Wisdom
ālokaḥ	Vision, light

Mastering saṁyama conjurs the dawning of wisdom.

There is an unspoken distance between our eyes and that with which we settle them upon. A myriad of history, emotional texture, and language can transform something as mundane as a tennis ball in the eyes of different people. It's for this reason, no one can touch the same water. No one can speak the same language. In the realm of materialism, we are essentially all alone.

Compare this with the fruits of *saṁyama*, which is a style of focus that transcends the material world. When using *saṁyama*, you're looking beyond what your eyes are capable of and through the objects you perceive. Because there's no material distinction, there's also no distance of history, emotional texture, or language between you.

We can see this technique come to life in the eyes and hearts of saints who see right through our race, class, and lifestyle. Sadhus who make eye contact with the soul instead of the body. Or among those who cross the Ganga river but don't witness the water.

Text 3.6

तस्य भूमिषु विनियोगः
tasya bhūmiṣu viniyogaḥ

tasya	Its, whose
bhūmiṣu	Stages
viniyogaḥ	Application, practice

Saṁyama is applied in various stages to our practice.

A talented musician will play so passionately, that they lose themselves to their instrument. Within seconds, all that can be perceived of them is their music. The musician would barely remember what happened. And you — you wouldn't remember seeing the musician. You would just remember the experience of the music. This is the act of the *saṁyama*.

In yoga, we attempt to apply this technique to our practice. The goal is for the practitioner and the practice to lose themselves to each other. All that gets left behind is our indigenous nature.

But *saṁyama* is just an artisan tool. It's simply a style of transcendental focus. And the depth of its clarity depends on the effort of its beholder. We could very easily use it to graze just the surface of materialism and catch a glance at something deeper. Perhaps to see the subtle, emotional welfare of a loved one. Something otherwise carefully hidden by their outward mood. But still we are an untold distance from seeing their soul.

Or we can apply it to our practice and witness unprecedented satisfaction. But suddenly the internet goes out and we are immersed in frustration. That reveals to us that the well wasn't deep enough. That what we witnessed was perhaps just the ego cleverly convincing us to bypass our attention back to ourselves.

It seems that the very last crossroad of *saṁyama* is the one between becoming one with everything or holding back to continue for service of love.

Text 3.7

त्रयमन्तरन्गं पूर्वेभ्यः
trayam-antarangaṁ pūrvebhyaḥ

trayam	Three
antar	Internal
aṅga	Limbs
pūrvebhyaḥ	Than the previous ones

These last three limbs, *dhāraṇā*, *dhyāna*, and *samādhi*, are more internal than their preceding five rungs.

An old sage may claim that even our emotions are external. Of course the body, the world, people, the streets are also external -- but the mind is as well. Our dreams, and myriad of thoughts; all external. Because behind the gift wrappings of these countless things is something way deep inside us. An entity without beginning or end.

We carefully decorate this entity layer by layer. First with the trappings of an individual perception. This comes harnessed with the five senses, a body that suffers, and a fear that keeps it running. Over time, it acquires a name, a list of short-term goals, responsibilities, perhaps even a relaxing desk job with a window view.

The most egotistical among us would consider the world outside that window as exclusively external. They'll gaze upon the strangers they'll never meet or the interests they'll never have and to them, everything closer than that is internal.

But as we broaden the context of our intelligence, and pierce through the superfluidity of the things we're decorated by – we quickly realize that the border between internal and external is an illusive line. It's a line drawn by the ego. In the same way Occam's razor aids the ego. We separate internal and external by dividing what we want to be permament versus what we want to change. The egoist wants the strangers to change, but could never accept that their heart could as well. In reality, everything changes.

The last three limbs are the doorway to the internal. A place undecorated by the ego or any such quality. Within such doors, the I and the actor become every face in the street, every movement near and far, and every passing tree.

Imagine what peace a falling leaf would hold if it knew it was the tree it fell from.

Text 3.8

तदपि बहिरङ्गं निर्बीजस्य
tadapi bahiraṅgaṁ nirbījasya

tadapi	That which also
bahir	External
aṅga	Limb
nirbīja	Seedless [samādhi]

But even these limbs are external compared to seedless *samādhi.*

There are two faces to enlightenment. The first is the one we see and celebrate. It is the personalized image of liberation. Such as the Buddha's image, the parables of Jesus, performing charity to the poor, or sharing fellowship with devotees. It is the one with direction, and an object to lead you.

The other is the nameless one. The one without cause or reason. The one that is impersonal and is present universally. The one we can't see and will never understand because of our perceptive limits. It is the Zen koan that has no answer.

The latter form of enlightenment are examples of seedless *samādhi* because there is no face to them. They exist just a fraction ahead of our ability to understand them. They are not born from a cause. That's why the sages called them seedless.

From the perspective of this causeless knowledge – everything is external. Even the doorway that leads within.

Text 3.9

व्युत्थाननिरोधसंस्कारयोः
अभिभवप्रादुर्भावौ निरोधक्षण चित्तान्वयो निरोधपरिणामः
vyutthāna-nirodha-saṁskārayoḥ abhibhava-prādurbhāvau
nirodhakṣaṇa cittānvayo nirodha-pariṇāmaḥ

vyutthāna	Outgoing, emerging
nirodha	Control, restraint
saṁskārayoḥ	Conscious imprints
abhibhava	Overpowering
prādurbhāvau	To manifest, appear
kṣaṇa	Instant, moment
nirodhakṣaṇa	Controlled moment
cittānvayo	Connected with
nirodha	consciousness
pariṇāmaḥ	Control, mastery
	Development

Nirodhah-pariṇāmaḥ is a transition of emerging into mastery while watching the imprints of the consciousness disappear. It is the mastery of that infinitesimal moment in change in connection with consciousness.

Imagine the soul covered in passing waves of identity. The soul will never be these identities, but they wash over it, back and forth so long as the soul experiences life. Most of us are incognizant of these changes, and therefore we hold on to one particular wave, one particular identity that could have been years, if not, generations old.

But sometimes we change in varying degrees. Maybe we pushed beyond the barriers of our identity. Maybe who we are can no longer exist in the world we witness. Whether it took generations or just a moment to develop, eventually everyone's identity is going to one day break.

Training ourselves to witness this subtle transition from illusion to control, or inertia to pure awareness – is a transition and a technique described by Patanjali. It is among four transitions he uses to describe the mechanisms of passing through the doorway to enlightenment. The first being the arousal of active awareness as opposed to passive awareness.

This transition is more than just coming into awareness. It's coming into awareness via a broader context. You coud say a bumblebee has awareness. But a broader awareness would have our loyal bee see herself as a cog in a living organism called a hive. And an enlightened bee would see her hive among an infinite ocean of interwoven species, places, seasons, and so on. The moment the bee realizes this, she experiences *nirodhah-pariṇāmaḥ*.

Text 3.10

तस्य प्रशान्तवाहिता संस्कारत्
tasya praśānta-vāhitā saṁskārat

tasya	Its
praśānta	Peaceful
vāhitā	Flow
saṁskāra	Subliminal impressions

If this state of *nirodhah-pariṇāmaḥ* flows undisturbed, it will write conscious imprints.

Our consciousness is like the music from a vinyl record. The grooves of the record are our subconscious imprints. These grooves are written by experience, trauma, joy, or sometimes inherited genetically. We live by them. There is very little that we do that didn't originate from these imprints.

We soon realize how little of an influence we have over our ideas, responses, interests, and choices. All of who we are and what we do is composed before we were consciously aware of it.

Take for example getting bit by a spider at a young age. The experience leaves an imprint where by, if unresolved, one continuously fears spiders. Eventually, there will be an entire life of choices composed from that one experience. Choices, including the fear itself, we will give to our children and their children. Entire languages will be authored by it. Entire cities will be developed from it. But these threads of influence end in *nirodhah-pariṇāmaḥ.*

Nirodhah-pariṇāmaḥ is the transition from mindless reaction to conscious will. It isn't a light switched on or off. It is a gradient of awareness versus reactiveness. By simply becoming aware, we overwrite the imprints of our preprogrammed nature with the imprints of awareness. Instead of mindless imprints that tease our animal instincts, we begin writing imprints that lead to our truth.

Moment by moment, we sculpt, sand, and polish the vehicle of our awareness to return to the essence of life. Our bodies become hollow. Our superfluous identities retreat, and our actions simplify to only that of which serves pure awareness.

One day, even the most mundane objects around us will be written by our awareness to return our attention to truth. And so the goal is to become poets of awareness. Those who write with the breath.

Text 3.11

सर्वार्थता एकाग्रातयोः
क्षयोदयौ चित्तस्य समाधिपरिणामः
sarvārthatā ekāgrātayoḥ kṣayodayau cittasya samādhi-pariṇāmaḥ

sarvārthata	On all objects
ekāgratā	Single-pointed focus
kṣaya	Destruction
udaya	To rise
citta	Of the mind
samādhi	Absolute absorption
pariṇāmaḥ	Transformation

Samādhi-pariṇāmaḥ is a transition state when all-pointedness decays and one-pointedness arises in the consciousness.

For every emotional pattern we adopt, life exhibits those patterns all around you. Even among the landscape. When we're depressed, we find it easy to describe the details in the ground around our feet. And when we are inspired, we somehow have the ability to describe the crevices in the moon and the stars abound. In short, how we feel is what the world essentially is. What we think is what the world becomes.

But our minds are the greatest of hoarders. We collect so many ideas, so many painful memories, so many details until our consciousness becomes obese. Our awareness begins to waddle with junk thought. And the world in response becomes maximalist and unnecessarily complicated. Our emotions are rarely a simple sense of joy, or a simple sense of pain. In this case, they are layers on top of layers of conflicting ideas and cosmopolitan emotions.

It's not just love anymore. It's guilt. It's confusion, happiness, fear, hate, and bliss all carefully shrink-wrapped around the origin of love. And the world in response manifests things like New York City.

And in one fantastic cycle, the city seeds these complicated layers in its city dwellers, and the city dwellers continue to patch on to its complexity. It is sometimes unfortunate that very few people have the opportunity to peer outside these unnecessary layers of complexity. To see fear as just fear. Or hate as just hate. Or love as just love. And as a result, realize a world that reflects the purest expression of the simplest of causes. To do so, to simplify, is a transition called *samādhi-pariṇāmaḥ.*

Samādhi-pariṇāmaḥ is the passage from all things to one thing. From the details of every single leaf to the root that feeds them all. Observing every individual effort in life as one unified effort from one unified being. It is a transition born from realizing that plurality is yet another illusion. And as we consciously consolidate to the lowest common denominator, even the skyscrapers and egos of the city reflect the wholesome simplicity of the heart.

Text 3.12

ततः पुनः
शातोदितौ तुल्यप्रत्ययौ चित्तस्यैकाग्रतापरिणामः
tataḥ punaḥ śātoditau tulya-pratyayau cittasya-ikāgratā-pariṇāmaḥ

tataḥ	Then
punaḥ	Again
śāntā	That which has been
uditau	subdued, the past
tulya	That which has arisen, the
pratyayau	present
cittasya	Similar
ekātmatā	Idea
pariṇāmaḥ	Of the mind
	Single-pointed
	Transition, development

Ekāgratā-pariṇāmaḥ is a transitional state where the consciousness' snapshot of presence is identical to presence.

Awareness arrives in two flavors. It can either be an acid wash of hallucinations or an untouched clarity. Either we see snapsots of memories fading one over the other, or we see no distance between presence and our perspective of it. The difference is in our sobriety.

But not just sobriety from common intoxicants. It is a sobriety from all things that intoxicate the soul, pollute the mind, and distract the heart. A subtle greed can be as intoxicating as alcohol. Lust can marionette our willpower as covertly as heroin. The idea of a separate self can be so captivating – that even thinking of ourselves as interdependent, eternal beings can be nauseating and terrifying.

When our will to live is untouched, virgin, and magnetically interwoven in the unscripted presence – then we experience *ekāgratā-pariṇāmaḥ.*

Ekāgratā-pariṇāmaḥ is the transition to presence in motion. A sacred place where the phenomenon of presence is unscathed by our perception.

Text 3.13

एतेन भूतेन्द्रियेषु धर्मलक्षणावस्था परिणामा व्याख्याताः
etena bhūtendriyeṣu dharma-lakṣaṇa-avasthā pariṇāmā vyākhyātāḥ

etena	By this
bhūtā	Elements
indriyeṣu	The senses
dharma	Nature, teaching,
lakṣaṇā	characteristics
avasthāḥ	Qualities
pariṇāma	Condition, state
vyākhyātāḥ	Change, evolution
	Explanation

These three transitions help us describe any object perceived by the senses; an object's nature, it's characteristics, and place in time.

There is an art to perception. It works very simply by noticing an object. There is our awareness of it. But then there's our transition to our full awareness of it. The distance between seeing an object and truly seeing an object can for many of us be impossibly wide.

That distance is composed by the three transitions we previously spoke of. Each one removing a layer of obfuscation. The first layer, our distractions and our presence is tranquilized by coming into focus. The second layer, our commentary and our plurality is quelled by our simplicity. And the final layer, the movement of time is pacified by our humility to keep pace with the present moment.

These three transitions; *nirodhah*, *ekāgratā*, *nirodhah* are the focal tools we adopt in varying degrees to reach awareness of any given person, place, or anywhere the imagination may roam. You could say, the transitions work the same way as the machine the optometrist uses to measure the eyes. Varying levers offering varying scopes of strength in your ability to see.

But their magnum opus is not the perception of a particular object. The real art is in using these tools to expand the scope of our total awareness. It is a subtle and beautiful art form to take notice of them working individually. First via the removal of disturbances, followed by single-minded focus, and the ability to to retain that consciousness through the passage of time.

Text 3.14

शान्तोदिताव्यपदेश्यधर्मानुपाती धर्मी

śāntodita-avyapadeśya-dharmānupātī dharmī

śānta	Ceased, the past
udita	Arisen, the present
avyapadeśya	The unnamed, the future
dharma	Nature, teaching,
anupātī	characteristics
dharmī	Is a consequence of
	The one who possesses nature

The past, present, and future are all natures that originate from a single nature.

The origin of time is our perception. Past, present, and future may infer something that was, is, or will be, but ultimately all direction of time is always in the eyes of its beholder. And the beholder of our perception is our context.

Context is the negative space that surrounds our point of focus. It fundamentally describes our point of focus sometimes better than our point of focus can describe itself. You could say, context is the commentary. And in most cases, the commentary is far greater than the subject itself. So overwhelming in fact that we don't actually see what we're seeing. Instead we only perceive the commentary.

Take for example a cow in a dance party compared to a cow in a farm. The latter would be easier to distinguish. The mind has already established what can and can not exist within a party or a farm. We've never seen a cow at a dance party so she might sneak in quite easily. Yet, even without a cow itself at the farm, just by the presence of a farm, we might easily mistake the presence of a cow.

This is why time, and our perception of time is relative to our context. Our commentary writes it. Not reality. From the perspective of awareness, past, present, and future are not real. They are simply written by the environment and the random nature of memory and intuition. They are essentially one phenomenon. As difficult as this may be to understand, these three states used to describe the phenomenon of time are of inherent equal value.

The only passage of time we experience is the timetraveling we perform with our awareness alone.

Text 3.15

क्रमान्यत्वं परिणामान्यतेवे हेतुः
kramānyatvaṁ pariṇāmānyateve hetuḥ

krama	Sequence
anyatvaṁ	Change
pariṇāma	Transformation
anyatva	Difference
hetu	The cause

The reason dinstinct changes exist is because of an underlying change in life's sequence.

The only sequence is awareness. The world around you, the passing birds, the smell of exhaust fumes, a light in the distance; is all awareness. There is no such thing as time, the passage of time, a past, present, or future. The only that changes is awareness. Awareness rises and sets. It clashes and it rejoices. And what you perceive with your five senses and rational mind is the consequence of this original awareness. Whatever medium awareness experiences, the world manifests.

This is the real sequence. This kind of sequence can not be perceived as linear. There are so many revolving vectors that shapeshift the aperture of our consciousness. This is why we abandon elementary ideas such as a past, present, and future.

Instead, we perceive ourselves living in an ocean of timeless energetic exchange. Every movement being the result of eternal actions repeating themselves indefinitely. These eternal actions collectively form an eternal being. And while we perform them, we are merely the atoms on the feet of this being.

For example, if you are to love, it was because you were loved, and the inspiration of loving will encourage you to love others. Who then is the living being? The greater living being is the expression of love. Our entire life is simply another wooden bead in a mala of lives it prays with. This greater living being chants upon those lives.

3.16

परिणामत्रयसंयमाततीतानागत ज्ञानम्

pariṇāmatraya-saṁyamāt-atītānāgata jñānam

pariṇāma	Change, evolution
traya	Three
saṁyamāt	Concentration, meditation,
atīta	and samadhi
anāgata	The past
jñānam	The future
	Knowledge

Complete absorption in the three transitions gives you knowledge of all cause and effect.

There is a very real way to measure reality. The measuring tools are the three transitions we spoke of previously. They measure a very real distance in the phenomenon we call life. The distance is a span where we have on one side an infinite layer of abstractions. Each layer more complicated than the one before. And on the other side we have pure undivided awareness. The distance begins as soon as we forget who we are. As soon as a moment loses its context, a distance appears. As soon as there is any notion of time or space, there is distance. We measure this distance by observing which of the three transitions we are among.

Once we understand these transitions, how they feel, how they instinctively lead us to return -- then we also begin seeing the same transitional distance in people and their personalities. We see it in society, in our jobs, even in mundane objects. Everything in life can be measured by its distance from reality.

And it is only within distance that cause and affect can occur. Otherwise in the sacred home of pure awareness, there is no movement. There is no action. Only until we separate and blur our attention from our eternal truth does the world come into being. The further along we are down the fractal of abstract truth, the more the world takes place.

3.17

शब्दार्थप्रत्ययामामितरेतराध्यासात्संकरः
तत्प्रविभागसंयमात् सर्वभूतरुतज्ञानम्

śabdārtha-pratyayāmām-itaretarādhyāsāt-saṁkaraḥ
tat-pravibhāga-saṁyamāt sarvabhūta-ruta-jñānam

artha	An object
pratyayāna	Of an idea
itaretarā	One with the other
adhyāsa	Imposing, superimposition
saṁkara	Mixing together
tat	These
pravibhāga	Distinctions
saṁyamāt	Concentration, meditation,
sarva	and samadhi
bhūta	All
ruta	Creatures
jñāna	Cries, sounds
	Knowledge

The consciousness operates by associating a word, the word's definition, and your personal understanding of what that word means to you to every given object. Each one of these three items is layered over the other and blended together. With the meditative practice of complete absorption, one can distinguish these layers and know what all creatures are saying.

Imagine the most beloved person in your life. There is the word that refers to them. There is brief description of them. And there is a catalogue of experiences that you've shared with them. At every given moment, these three elements are cascading over and into each other obscuring who that beloved person really is. But none of these three descriptions are actually them.

Your beloved is not simply a word, a brief description, or a cloud of experiences. Those three elements are just shadows of their identity. The real act of knowing someone arrives when we discover our love for them. This is because love is an act of total absorption, or *samyama*, which leaves us speechless. And in the wake of that silence, we have room to listen.

Unlike using just our ears or senses or memories, *samyama* allows you to listen to the fountainhead of their soul. It is a place where your beloved speaks before a narrative, before the senses can translate meaning. *Samyama*, just like love, transcends all language barriers. When you are completely absorbed, you realize that every living creature, every breeze, and ocean is saying something to you. And its message comes well before whatever words there may be.

Text 3.18

संस्कारसाक्षात्करणात् पूर्वजातिज्ञानम्
saṁskāra-sākṣātkaraṇāt pūrva-jāti-jñānam

saṁskāra	Subliminal impressions
sākṣāt	Before one's eyes, direct
karaṇāt	Experience
sākṣātkaraṇat	Direct experience
pūrva	Previous
jāti	Birth, class, caste
pūrva	āti,"Previous birth
jñānam	Knowledge

By bringing our thought patterns to our attention, we become aware of previous births.

Most of what we do is mindless reaction. Reactions prewritten by *samskaras* which are grooves cut into our consciousness. These grooves are neurological synapses that form pathways throughout the brain. These pathways connect phenomenon to reaction.

When we hear a loud crash, we associate a reaction to it. That reaction becomes burned into our subconsciousness, and every time the sound returns, so does our prerecorded reaction.

As your yoga practice deepens, you'll soon discover that many of your samskaras weren't created by you. The deeper ones were likely genetically or emotionally inherited from your parents and community. There are even more subtle samskaras that were formed during the advent of your species. For example, possessing a vertebrae comes with its own *samskaras* that induce certain fears and responses that resulted in the evolutionary development of this particular bone structure.

Once we develop a context for who we were before the body, before the physiological adaptation of the mind, we can then observe the evolutionary call and response our bodies went through. We can see every birth. We can see every triumph, fear, and preference. We can observe the bodies that served our interests, and those that didn't.

Ultimately, we can see the trial and error that reflects our earnestness to communicate. We can see the message. And the myriad of mediums we have physiologically adopted in order to speak it.

Text 3.19

प्रत्ययस्य परचित्तज्ञानम्
pratyayasya para-citta-jñānam

pratyayasya	From the ideas
para	Of others
citta	Of the minds
jñānam	Knowledge

From understanding the architecture of thought, you will understand other's minds.

We all want the same things in life. Every living being does. There is very little that differentiates us. The decisions you make are not too distant from the decisions everyone else has made or ever will. The only thing that does differentiate us is what context we have of the world when we made those decisions.

Context is the easiest way to describe enlightenment. If the context of your observation is great, it is because you see a bigger picture and all the events that lead up to and surround that moment in time.

As you start leaning towards this greater context, your actions become larger, and your ideas last longer. As your context deepens, you will understand the mindsets of others with smaller contexts. Much in the same way, a mother won't fight back with violence when their child has a tantrum. The mother understands the bigger picture. She knows that the child's tantrum comes from a small, short-distance context.

You can see short-distance context in election cycles, corporate advertising, and religious fanaticism. Where people with a relative degree of enlightenment are using their ability to coerce and manipulate others with a short-distance context. It's why some of us eat meat. They believe their long-distance context justifies killing those with a shorter-distance. Luckily, we can rest assured that anyone who has to demand such an authority to teach has just authority and nothing to teach.

The only thing we can actually learn is that which carries us back to truth. Everything else is mindless details. When we understand this dualist nature of power versus surrender, truth versus abstraction, long-distance versus short-distance, the entire architecture of the consciousness unfolds.

Text 3.20

न च तत् सालम्बनं तस्याविषयी भूतत्वात्

na ca tat sālambanaṁ tasya-aviṣayī bhūtatvāt

na	Not
ca	And
tat	That
sa	His
ālambanam	Support, the underlying
tasyaḥ	Its
aviṣayī	Not the object
bhūtatvāt	Because it is

We read the effect and fruition of other's thoughts, not the actual specific thoughts themselves.

To every individual, the things we experience can never be shared with someone else. Even if we were standing in the same place, pointing at the same thing.

This is because we exist in an exclusive bubble of individual experience. Our descriptions are only echoes of the actual objects themselves. We don't react to what the world is. We react to our frivolous sandcastles of the world. The details of our homes, our friends, and families are ghosts compared to the people and places themselves.

So when the yogi reads someone else's mind or merely listens to them speak, the words themselves are irrelevant. What they're actually listening to is the subtler aspect of their speaker, their emotional body or even deeper, their soul. When people speak, the words are the furthest after effect to whatever they might be trying to say.

Much in the same way, the teachings of great gurus can't be quoted because their most important teachings are their presence alone.

Text 3.21

कायरूपसंयमात् तत्ग्राह्यशक्तिस्तम्भे चक्षुः
प्रकाशासंप्रयोगेऽन्तर्धानम्
kāya-rūpa-saṁyamāt tat-grāhyaśakti-stambhe cakṣuḥ
prakāśāsaṁprayoge-'ntardhānam

kāya	Of the body
rūpa	Form
saṁyamāt	Concentration, meditation,
tat	and samadhi
grāhya	That
śakti	To be grasped, perceptible
stambhe	Power, capacity
arhtaḥ	On the obstruction
cakṣuḥ	Impediment
prakāśa	Eye
asaṁprayoge	Light
antardhānam	No connection
	Invisibility

Total absorption affects our body form by giving it power to be suspended in the eye's visual stimulii as invisible.

One of the most difficult things to give up is a sense of identity. Our identity is like an anchor in an ever changing world. The world can change overnight, but you don't have to because you can just close your eyes, and say, I am still me. I don't change.

It's far easier to tell yourself who you are, then negotiate who we are with the world. This is what leads us to narcissism because it hurts to let the world define you, and it hurts even more to accept what it says we are.

Instead of finding confidence from very real things like our non-dualist breath, we seek a superficial confidence in our identity, our skills, and interests. The bigger the ego, the more real estate it requires. The more real estate it requires, the less it can exist among nature. And so it's very easy to spot these types of creatures. They demand large homes, large front lawns, they call the police often. But as we learn how to absorb ourselves with love or meditation, we realize that who we are is transient. Our entire identity comes and goes like water in our hands.

If we can accept this truth, and let go of the need to self-identify — we won't need a large home. Instead of a front lawn, we can let nature grow there. You might even find that your perseverance and compassion are stronger than the police. Eventually, nature surrounds you. You become invisible.

Text 3.22

सोपक्रमं निरुपक्रमं च कर्म तत्संयमातपरान्तज्ञानम् अरिष्टेभ्यो वा
sopa-kramaṁ nirupa-kramaṁ ca karma tatsaṁyamāt-aparāntajñānam ariṣṭebhyo vā

krama	Sequence, succession
sopakramaṁ	Based on the process
nirupa	Without form, empty
nirupakramaṁ	A process without form
ca	And
karma	Physics, cause and effect
tat	That
saṁyamāt	Performing saṁyama
aparānta	Death
jñāna	Knowledge
ariṣṭa	Fate, omens
ibhya	Its
vā	Or

Karma comes and goes fulfilling an inevitable nature. Complete absorption in karma or in its milestones allows you to know when even death will arise.

Karma finds its best explanation in modern physics. That energy can't be created or destroyed, only altered. That all things in motion, continue at the same velocity. So we can say, people who are abused becomes abusers. People who are loved become lovers. There are patterns to karma.

Patterns we demonstrate in our life. Patterns we inherited from our ancestors. And in a much greater way, our entire life is just one small milestone in a pattern that takes generations to develop and fade away. Whether its hate, love, enlightenment, music, dance, or fire — every action has its spark, growth, and decay. When we become completely absorbed in the art of karma, we see the simplicity of something like an ocean's wave in everything. We see the light wash over the world and recede. We see where someone's anger came from and how long it will last. We can tell how many generations it will take to recover from the suffering of war. And just as all things begin and end, so do we. Without the ego to intervene, we become aware of when that very moment will be. And we welcome it with joy.

Text 3.23

मैत्र्यदिषु बलानि
maitry-adiṣu balāni

maitrī	Friendliness
ādiṣu	Etc.
balāni	Strength

Friendliness, etc. brings strength.

Life is uncertain. Period. And if uncertainty makes you scared, then your life is going to be terrifying. If uncertainty causes you no reaction at all, then your life will never be interesting. Your relationship with not knowing is quintessential to your spiritual development.

Uncertainty is the last human experience you will have before enlightenment. It is also the direct effect of performing *samyama*, or complete absorption in meditation. It should be seen, always, as a gift. You can give uncertainty to your loved ones, and you are giving them the freedom to be themselves. You can give uncertainty to yourself saying, I don't know who I am, and you are giving yourself room to grow and adapt.

Just like any gift, the best way to receive it is with friendliness. By receiving uncertainty with friendliness, you invoke a healthy curiosity to interact with reality, or what we call truth. Because truth doesn't reveal itself in dogma. It can never, and will never be recorded or demonstrated. Even if the greatest teacher pointed it out for you, his or her finger would simply be in the way.

This is because truth can only be witnessed. And when truth reveals itself, there is no commentary or logic that can define it. It just is. And therefore, to experience the most basic concept of reality, to have the experience of being alive, we have to be able to accept not knowing. And if we approach not knowing with friendliness, then we develop the strongest means of interacting with this briefly held life.

Text 3.24

बलेषु हस्तिबलादीनी
baleṣu hastibalādīnī

baleṣu	On the power, strength
hasti	Elephant
balā	Strength of
ādīnī	Et cetera

Total absorption in strength brings the strength of an elephant.

The only thing preventing you from being the elephant, the mountain, the eternity of the sky, or the ethereal breeze is the restriction you self-impose with the words, I am.

Even if your goals are something more reasonable. Perhaps just ten kilos more in a deadlift, one hour longer with your practice, or one more day trying to be sober – the only thing standing in your way is the person you were. When you shed that self-identity, you can be who you are.

Fear is ego. Limitations are ego. When love replaces ego, then we have achieved pure awareness. From this sacred place, our strength is unparalleled. We become as strong as the elephant.

Text 3.25

प्रवृत्त्यालोकन्यासात् सूक्ष्माव्यावहितविप्रकृष्टज्ञानम्
pravṛttyāloka-nyāsāt sūkṣmā-vyāvahita-viprakṛṣṭa-
jñānam

pravṛtti	Cognition, higher sense
āloka	activity
nyāsā	Light
sūkṣma	By projecting, directing
vyavahita	Subtle
viprakṛṣṭa	Concealed, hidden
jñāna	Remote
	Knowledge

When we know how to direct consciousness as light, we understand the subtle, the hidden, and even things far away.

The night reflects the natural state of the universe. It is the quiet and dark presence of things at rest. But the day, the waking life, evolution, and photosyntheses are all biproducts of the sun. Its influence reverberates around the Earth in the form of lightning, wildfires, electrical synapses in the brain and vertebrae. Each expression of light is something smaller, creative, but ultimately composed of the same material.

Awareness is identical to light. Whatever we know of light we can apply to consciousness. Whatever we don't understand about awareness we can learn from light.

Our total lack of awareness is also a natural state. It is the quiet and dark presence of non-action. But the senses, waking life, evolution, and photosyntheses are all biproducts of awareness. Its influence reverberates around the Earth in the form of living beings, communication, and for the individual; music and dancing. Each expression of consciousness is something smaller, creative, but ultimately composed of the same material.

Essentially all matter is composed of light just as all matter is composed of awareness. They are both a material object and a velocity through four dimensional space.

Whomsoever we direct our practice towards, whether it be the guru, the sun, or *Isvara*, the true origin will always be fleetingly greater than our focus. The yogi accepts this impossible goal, and instead, bows towards the feet of whomsoever is closest. And within them the light goes on.

Text 3.26

भुवज्ञानं सूर्येसंयमात्
bhuva-jñānaṁ sūrye-saṁyamāt

bhuvana	World, realm
jñāna	Knowledge
sūrye	On the sun
saṁyamāt	By saṁyama

By meditation on the sun, one understands cosmic organization.

Our beloved planet, its wavering oceans, and crawling mountains were born from fire. This entire planet, and a handful of similar planets encircle an example of the fire they come from; the sun.

Because of the proximity to their origin, the light alone is capable of nourishing life amidst total infinite emptiness. This cosmic movement isn't isolated to the stars. There are parallels riddled throughout our day. The way we orbit around beliefs, the way we orbit around suffering, the way we rally around love.

This is because every idea is a living being that holds its own gravity. Anything lesser is drawn to it. So when we stare at the sun, we see the sun in our beliefs. We see the world that gravitates to our intentions. We are reminded of the light that nourishes our gardens. We are reminded that whatever holds the cosmos together, is intrinsically what holds everything in life together.

Text 3.27

चन्द्रे ताराव्यूहज्ञानम्
candre tāravyūha-jñānam

candre	The moon
tāra	Star
vyūha	Arrangement
jñānam	Knowledge
tāra vyūha jñāna	Knowledge concerning arrangement of stars

By meditation on the moon, one understands the arrangement of the stars.

When we turn away from the sun, the night reveals a myriad of stars. Stars that are foreign and impossible to understand if it were not for the moon. Which acts as a guide for what exists beyond the sun's influence.

What we discover is an ocean of other galaxies and other systems. Just as when we turn away from the blinding ideas we gravitate around, we discover a sea of other beliefs. Billions of energetic systems like our own, spiraling around their own respective dharmas. We realize that no matter how genuine our system is, there are infinite others just like our own.

The stars teach us that all realizations are one. Whether your path is to believe in God or not to believe in God, to follow a mantra, a prayer, a master, or poverty — all paths revolve around identical suns in mirrored places.

The only difference we have is in the distance we hold from our origin or *yoga*. Which is neither a star or a place, but an origin our awareness manifests from. The further away we are from our awareness, the more unique we believe we are, and the more entitled we feel we are to our ideas. Vice versa, at the fountainhead of conscious realization, you would not be able to distinguish between Muslim, Christian, B'Hai, Krisna, human, mammal, rock, or element. The stars teach us the beauty of plurality. Just as they teach us about the unity of light.

Text 3.28

ध्रुवे तद्गतिज्ञानम्
dhruve tadgati-jñānam

dhruve	The north star
tat	Its, their [the stars]
gati	Movement
jñānam	Knowledge

Meditative absorption on the north star brings knowledge on the movement of stars.

Staring northward, the entire solar system seems to revolve around the north star. In Hindu mythology, the north star is referred to as Dhruva. Named after the beloved devotee who at the age of five, was broken-heartedly rejected from his royal home.

As a result, he ventured deep into the jungle to find God. For six months, Dhruva abstained from food and water, his mind fixed exclusively on God. His tapas shook the heavens, and the Lord appeared before him asking what he could reward him with; worldly or heavenly pleasures, or even complete liberation.

But Dhruva no longer had any personal desire. In fact, he completely forgot what his original intention was. Instead, he asked only for a life in the memory of the Lord.

Thus so, Vishnu granted his wish by making him into a celestial body that transcended even the cycle of the big bang. Although there are trillions of stars -- the one law all things abide by is the gravity of devotion. And if we know how to identify true devotion, we also discover that the entire universe revolves around this concept. Thus so, just like the northern star, if you know devotion, you will always be able to find your way around the world without a map.

Text 3.29

नाभिचक्रे कायव्यूहज्ञानम्

nābhicakre kāyavyūha-jñānam

nābhi	Navel
cakre	Upon the wheel
kāya	Physical body
vyūha	Arrangement
jñānam	Knowledge

Meditating on the navel, you will understand body's arrangement.

The navel is designed by a noble echo. An echo carried by a sequence of life from the very source of life itself. It is the end of a long chain that connects the very first being to our existence.

Within this chain, we taught ourselves how to survive. How to fly and sometimes camoflauge. Through this chain, we found all sorts of awareness. We learned sight. We learned infared, music, and magnetism. New meaning. New expression. Every individual life sweetening their own little aum.

The belly button is a long and loyal line from the source of life. A mala of lives strung together through time. Each individual bead a being, a lover, a mother, and a memory. And now here we are again. Again from this navel comes forth our hands and brain, our skeleton and eyes, the spoken word and our aching hearts. All as it were from an ancient echo to the helm of the navel.

When we truly meditate on the navel, we see this succession of life. We watch evolution unfold in a curious way. Because outside of our will to survive there's something else. Something more. Within this echo is also a calling. It's found in the way we pray, in the dawn mantra of birds in flight, and the sound of water. There is, among this echo, a will to surrender in love.

Text 3.30

कन्ठकूपे क्षुत्पिपासा निवृत्तिः
kaṇṭha-kūpe kṣutpipāsā nivṛttiḥ

kaṇtha	Throat
kūpa	Pit, hollow
kṣudh	Hunger
pipāsā	Thirst
nivṛttiḥ	Cessation, cease

By meditating on the pit of the throat, hunger and thirst will end.

Hunger is a process, and starvation requires at least a few days to be harmful. But most of us have never been in a position of starvation so just the symbolic gesture of hunger, missing a meal or two, instinctively invokes the same emotional intensity had our lives been threatened at gunpoint.

We immediately welcome our most primitive instincts, our fight or flight habits, to commandeer our soul. What's more, the world is aware of this and profiteers from harmful foods just because their food is more accessible to people who don't understand hunger.

There is more nutrition in a deep breath of wild forest air then there is in any fast food, anywhere on the planet. In our meditation, if we observe the energetic line drawn from our lower intestine to the bottom of our throat, we can see how the pangs of hunger emerge, and where they come from. By understanding this process, we can separate our emotional response from what is a very simple and usually a harmless biological process.

The yogi cures their own hunger by acceptance. But we cure others hunger by ensuring they have something to eat.

Text 3.31

कूर्मनाड्यां स्थैर्यम्
kūrma-nāḍyāṁ sthairyam

kūrma	Tortoise
nāḍyām	Subtle channel
kūrma-nāḍī	Energy channel near sternum
sthairyam	Steadiness

By meditating on the tortoise channel, steadiness is attained.

Nadis are the subtle veins of energy that flow throughout our body. Some ancient texts cite 72,000 different lines, diminishing in power the further they travel from the center of the body. Some of the veins connect to other worlds beyond the crown chakra and are used at the time of death. In some places, thousands of nadis intersect into power centers we understand as *chakras*. However, wheresoever they cross, these are called *marmas*.

The entire system is carefully mapped. We employ these maps in acupuncture, chiropractic philosophy, Chinese medicine, and very much so in the alignment of yoga asana and pranayama.

The *kūrma nāḍi* is a very particular pathway located at the bottom of the trachea between both bronchii. During a breath cycle, it is very easy to notice the lungs expanding, or the soft white noise from our nostrils. This is the epicenter of our breath awareness. It is where consciousness greets the shores of the living being.

When we focus on this particular nadi, we begin with something easy to hold on to; the rise and fall of the lungs. But just below this layer is the subtle texture for how we breathe. Within each inhalation and exhalation a story could be read of our entire life. More so from the series of lives that lead to us. If we could zoom in, magnify, and elongate the style of any given breath, you would be able to read the story of your destiny.

However, the truest details of such a breath lie even far below these nuances. They dwell in the energetic *nadis*. An experience that requires a hunter's patience to acquire. By perfecting this observation, we are essentially microtuning the crown connection between body and consciousness.

Text 3.32

मूर्धज्योतिषि सिद्धदर्शनम्
mūrdha-jyotiṣi siddha-darśanam

mūrdha	Head, crown of head
jyotiṣi	Light
siddha	Perfected one
darśanam	Vision

By meditating on the light around our head, we can see all of the perfected souls.

Enlightenment is not limited to any religion or education. It is a very real experience that is achieved by thousands of humble souls every generation. The process begins with broadening the context of the I am. Where *I am* no longer implies just this body with its borders being the flesh.

Instead this, *I am*, is the entire living world. The passing clouds, the myriad of people, the rain, the sound of cars — all of this to an enlightened being is -- *I am*.

They are everything, everything that was, and everything that will ever be. Their eyes become ancient. No longer is the world behind those eyes an individual in a specific time period with specific fears and disinterests. Instead, they are the fountainhead of consciousness before consciousness became an individual. When truth was still an experience and not a commodity.

This experience is impossible to see while we are coveted by materialism. Who can enjoy the pleasure of fresh greens while they fiend for sugar? Materialism just like sugar is a mental disease. It overrides your natural propensity to see value so long as your bodily mechanism is in desperate need. As so, materialism operates as a drug. It keeps you fiending, sleeping, and moving on autopilot.

Once we start the purification process, healing the body with nutritious foods and the soul with sweetened mantra, the body with yoga asana and the mind with meditation – we begin to see a light around our head. It's only from this experience, that we can begin to notice the light around others. No one can see in others, their light, until they see their own. And when they do, their entire rational for whom they associate with and why immediately changes.

Text 3.33

प्रातिभाद्वा सर्वम्
prātibhād-vā sarvam

prātibhā	By intuition
vā	Or
sarvam	All, everything

Or meditation on intuition brings knowledge of everything.

Consciousness is like water to the Ganges river. Before our individual awareness has a name, an identity, and a pathway, it is just water. The water of the Ganges just like our consciousness is not limited to this particular path, but it can be found in the passing clouds, in every ocean, and in every living creature. But unlike water, consciousness is aware. It is the force that perceives. It is the source of knowledge.

Historically, living beings have accessed this tap through meditation, drugs, trauma, and the creative arts. Just as the physical body evolves, so does our individual consciousness, and its direction is towards this greater, more pervasive awareness.

There have been individuals who either by grace or willpower have discovered means of connecting with this creative origin. Plato, Leonardo Da Vinci, Isaac Newton, Nikola Tesla, and Albert Einstein, who were all coincidentally vegetarian, forwarded exponentially our scientific perception of the universe. They had access to information that took hundreds of years past their death to prove.

Likewise, across the planet, humanity has made independent discoveries of the same things. Things like ship building, writing, astrology, calculus, and evolution were all discovered independently by different peoples around the same time periods. We all have access to the same source.

Thus so, if one meditates on this creative source — they come into contact with all knowledge, the source of awareness; all answers, all scientific discoveries, every variation of artistic expression.

Text 3.34

हृडये चित्तसंवित्

hrḍaye citta-saṁvit

hr̥daya	Heart
citta	The mind
saṁvit	Understanding, precise knowledge

Meditation on the heart reveals knowledge of the mind.

There is nothing intellectual about enlightenment. Enlightenment begins and ends with the heart. And an enlightened heart is love. A love that is purely devotional. A loves for the sake of love. Something that has no interest in receiving any sort of response for its efforts. When you can interact with someone without needing something from them, then you can truly listen to them. When you can interact with your life as a whole without needing anything from life as a whole, then you can truly live.

Love is therefore the key to a sober reality. A reality where by this world is shared equally with others because they can see themselves in others. For an enlightened heart, there is no differentiation between this so called I and this so called other. If we understand the heart, we understand the mind, we see the world outside the self, and we touch the doorway of enlightenment.

Text 3.35

सत्त्वपुरुषायोः अत्यन्तासंकीर्णयोः
प्रत्ययाविशेषोभोगः
परार्थत्वात्स्वार्थसंयमात् पुरुषज्ञानम्
sattva-puruṣāyoḥ atyantā-saṁkīrṇayoḥ
pratyayāviśeṣo-bhogaḥ
para-arthat-vāt-sva-arthasaṁyamāt puruṣa-jñānam

sattva	Purity, of the intellect
puruṣa	Of the true self, pure
atyantā	consciousness
a-saṁ-kīrṇayoḥ	Complete, very, extremely
pratyayaḥ	aṁ-kīrṇayoḥ,"Different,
aviśeṣaḥ	distinct
bhogaḥ	Idea, notion
para	Nondistinction, non-subject
artha	Pleasure, experience
vāt	External, of other
para-arthat-vāt	Object, goal, matter
sva	Instead of
artha	Having the nature to exist for
svartha	other
saṁyamāt	Belong to oneself, reflexive
puruṣa	Object, desire, goal
jñānam	For itself
	From samyaṁa
	Pure consciousness, the
	universal self
	Knowledge

The most enlightened intellect and pure consciousness are completely different things. Even the purest, most nondistinctive experience is still just a shadow of pure consciousness. By meditating on this this difference, we see how pure consciousness becomes the shadow of itself, enlightened intellect.

Who we are is a very illusive moving target. We are only the things we surround ourselves with. Change any one of those things, and we change. At the core of all these changing things is what is recognized as pure consciousness. Pure consciousness works by perceiving the world, and the world responds by reflecting the perceiver.

So by witnessing pain, we become pain. By witnessing joy, we become joy. For pure consciousness, these emulations come and go as soon as the experience comes and goes. But unlike pure consciousness, our minds hold on to these identities, sometimes several years after witnessing what created them.

This is how we develop an unrealistic self. So despite being surrounded by joy, we're still in pain. Or despite being surrounded by pain, we're in some false sense of joy. There begins a drift between the present moment and who we are. This is parallel to the same drift that exists between the present moment and our perception of it.

The further we drift behind sudden presence, the faker our perception becomes, the faker we become. This is why the highest aspiration of meditation is to reach this fountainhead of consciousness, effectually ending any drift. But the mind alone can never actually reach it. As close as it may ever get, it is still just a shadow of pure awareness. In this sutra, Patanjali is essentially saying, don't mistake the fountainhead for the source of water.

Text 3.36

ततः प्रातिभस्रावाणवेदनाअदर्शाअस्वादवार्ता जायन्ते
tataḥ prātibha-srāvāṇa-vedana-ādarśa-āsvāda-vārtā jāyante

tataḥ	Thence, from this
prātibha	Intuition
śrāvaṇa	Hearing
vedana	Touch
ādarśa	Seeing
āsvāda	Tasting
vārtā	Odor, Smelling
jāyante	Are born, engenders

Thus so, higher consciousness produces higher, transcendental hearing, touch, vision, taste, and smell.

In a popular zen koan, a man is chased by tigers through the woods. He slips off a cliff, but manages to grab hold of a dead branch jutting from the side. Several more tigers pace hungrily at the bottom of the cliff, while the other tigers wait hungrily at the top. The branch he's holding on to starts to break. And it was at this time, that he noticed beautiful red strawberries growing on the side of the cliff. He quickly picks and eats one. It was the most delicious strawberry he ever had!

What makes that strawberry so beautiful and so sweet is not so much the strawberry. It's because there is no drift between the present moment and his perception of it.. He has no time to have a narrative about this experience. No time to compare it to anything else he's ever witnessed. And so he lives absolutely for the moment; his very last moment on Earth.

Even though the strawberry is naturally sweet, its real sweetness is much deeper than taste. Here his soul is being satiated through the ceremonious usage of the taste. But the real sweetness is derived from his presence. It is a satisfaction unparalleled to anything in the material world. Because instead of watering the superfluous details of our life, we water the roots – our soul. As it is infinitely more satisfying to fulfill the soul than it is the senses.

Text 3.37

ते समाधवुपसर्गाव्युत्थाने सिद्धयः

te samādhav-upasargā-vyutthāne siddhayaḥ

te	It, they [the powers]
samādaui	Those who are enlightened
upasargā	Obstacles
vyutthāna	Outgoing, materially-invested
siddhayaḥ	Perfected powers

These special powers are obstacles to enlightenment, and attainments to the material mind.

Imagine yourself in a game. A game by which there's no way to win. You can only at best make small achievements. But it never takes long to end up right where you started. The reason we play is because it is the culture to do so. No one questions it.

But let's imagine one day you do. Your question leads you to realize that you're just playing a game. And you start noticing little breaks and tears in the game. You realize how predictable the world is. How the mind ultimately has no individuality and just reflects whatever surrounds it. You realize that even the rules by which everyone plays by are changing constantly. Yet nobody is aware of this. Because everyone is still playing. It's simply the culture to do so.

But if we know where the game is broken, we can very easily break it even more. And while we know how it breaks, we know exactly how to manipulate the system. The irony however, is that the only reason one would ever have to manipulate the game, is to keep playing it. And should they keep playing it, they will very quickly forget how it breaks.

The body and the mind together are the game. These sophisticated tools are incredible, but they are not aware. They have no consciousness. Just as your computer or your car equally have no awareness. They are simply extensions. Should you want to know who the driver is one day, you will have to abandon all the fruits that come with this quest. Hold on to just one fruit, and you'll have to start all over again.

Text 3.38

बद्न्हकारणशैथिल्यात् प्रचारसंवेदनाच्च चित्तस्य परशरीरावेशः
bandha-kāraṇa-śaithilyāt pracāra-saṁvedanācca cittasya paraśarīrāveśaḥ

bandha	Bondage, attachment
kāraṇa	Cause
śaithilya	From the loosening
pracāra	Passageways, channels
saṁvedana	Precise knowledge of
ca	And
citta	Mind
para	Another
śarīra	Body
āveśa	Entering into

By relaxing the cause of attachments, one gains knowledge of moving the consciousness and entering through another's body.

By becoming hyper observational to your consciousness, you gain psychic access to the world around you. You realize that these thoughts were never actually yours. That the thoughts themselves stem from the world around you. That every conscious and inanimate being are just satellites of consciousness, bouncing back and forth, traveling around the universe, spreading for generations.

Wherever you are, that is the state of your mind. Whatever you associate with, that is who you are. No being's consciousness is unique. We're all the same reflective mirrors absorbing the same world around us.

It's with this perception, that one can begin interacting with others on a much deeper level. We can begin planting seeds in each other, influencing others by our karma, our inspiration; or directly inhabiting someone. Entering into the mind of someone else has to be done from a vantage point higher than our own small mind. But it can be experienced very easily through things like kirtan music where for just a moment, we share a higher consciousness, and the music is our connection. We are then controlled by a greater satellite.

This is because devotion dissolves the ego that separates us. We become each other. Love, by its very nature operates in the same way. Lovers can act through each other. A guru can speak through her students. The universe can sing through our joy.

Text 3.39

उदानजयाअत् जलपण्खकण्टकादिष्वसङ्गोऽत्क्रान्तिश्च

udāna-jayāat jala-paṇkha-kaṇṭakādiṣv-asaṅgo-'tkrāntiśca

udāna	One of the pranas, vital air
jayāt	energy
jala	Mastery
paṇkha	Water
kaṇṭaka	Mud
ādiṣu	Thorn
asaṅgaḥ	Etc.
utkrānti	Noncontact
ca	Levitation, ascension
	And

Mastering udana, one can levitate over even water, mud, and thorns.

Without the aid of modern science and psychology, the most brilliant minds of ancient India contemplated the laws of energy. They believed that the sun was the source of all energy called *prana* in sanskrit , and that from this source, all living beings transformed prana into five varied types of energy that govern our bodies.

They are called *prana*, *samana*, *vyana*, *apana*, and *udana*. *Prana* is the fuel. *Samana* transforms the fuel to energy. *Vyana* circulates the energy throughout the body. *Apana* releases the waste material. And *udana*, the final product, offers us our expression and enthusiasm.

In this sutra, Patanjali refers specifically to *udana*. If we can simply take a step back from our circus of thoughts, we can observe the growth and maintenance of enthusiasm within us. This is our *udana*, our expressive energy. With careful mastery of *udana*, we can be joyful for the sake of joy and not for any particular circumstance. Look at a joy like that — you can barely touch the ground.

Text 3.40

समानजयाज्ज्वलनम्
samāna-jayāt-jvalanam

samāna	Metabolic energy
jayāt	Mastery
jvalanam	Effulgence, fire

Mastering *samāna*, gives one radiance.

Miners would bring canary birds into the mines because the bird would respond to a gas leak before they were consciously aware of it. Our breath is like a canary bird in the mines of our consciousness. From the breath alone, we can observe how the world effects us before we are consciously aware of it. And by mastering the breath, we take ownership of our means of awareness.

Samāna is a particular type of energy that is found in the distance between an inhalation and an exhalation. It's mastered by suspending the breath. The act of finding calm when our lungs no longer respond. It is an experience that pervades into every corner of the consciousness. Suspending the breath is the act of balancing our entire life on the subtle nerve endings of our lungs, and from it, our attention hardens, and our presence becomes effulgent. The pause in our breath becomes a light to our presence.

Text 3.41

श्रोत्राअकाशयोः संबन्धसंयमात् दिव्यं श्रोत्रम्
śrotra-ākāśayoḥ saṁbandha-saṁyamāt divyaṁ śrotram

śrotra	Ear, hearing organ
ākāśa	Ether, space
saṁbandha	Connection
saṁyama	By concentration, meditation, and samadhi
divya	Divine, higher
śrotram	Hearing

By meditation on the relationship between the ear and substratum of sound, one acquires divine hearing.

The ego operates exactly the same way any other particular body part of ours functions. White blood cells, the heart, the endocrine system — none of these are conscious by themselves. Just like the ego, they seek to self-preserve, self-protect, and expand their power. None of them are aware of it. The only reason our egos don't consume us into total narcissism is because we have an awareness that hopefully prevents this. Whether we were aware of it or not, at some point we said, this isn't exactly me.

There was definitely a moment in our lives when we looked at our feverish self-interest, our self-preservation and realized one or two things. One, that it's actually going to be alright. We're going survive, and we shouldn't feel threatened. The second, is that we may have also realized that this fear driven thirst for survival comes at the cost of those we love. The more we hunger to protect ourselves, the more we exclude those we love.

That mindset excludes everything. The ego builds your thought process by this decree -- so long as it doesn't serve the ego directly, it doesn't exist. And so if there are people who only love you but don't serve your power, you will never meet them. If the Earth only serves your soul, but not your ego's thirst for power, it will get covered in parking lots.

That is unless an awareness intervenes. The awareness reminds the ego just as the body does to the heart, that there's blood to be shared by all. Then suddenly we can see those loved ones or the Earth or strangers — or literally anything outside of what serves us.

In music, God can be heard in the space between the notes, but the ego is forever poised to fill this space with itself. So if you can abandon this character who listens, and just listen — then the full expression of the music can be heard. This could be understood as divine hearing.

Text 3.42

कायाकाशयोः संबन्धसंयमात् लघुतूलसमापत्तेश्चाअकाश गमनम्
kāyākāśayoḥ saṁbandha-saṁyamāt laghu-tūla-samāpatteśca-ākāśa gamanam

kāya	The body
ākāśa	Ether, space, substratum
saṁbandha	Connection
saṁyama	By concentration, meditation, and samadhi
laghu	Light, lightning
tūla	Cotton
samāpatti	Intense concentration
ca	And
ākāśa	Ether, space, substratum
gamanam	Movement, passage

By practicing saṁyama on the relationship between the body and its essence, you will become as weightless as light and cotton.

Consciousness pervades everything. Consciousness is the essence of everything. With the greatest of microscopes, you will only ever see yourself. With the greatest of telescopes, you will only ever see yourself. When two zen monks watched a flag whipping in the wind, one asked to the other, what is moving, the flag or the wind? The other monk replied, only mind is moving.

Only the consciousness exists. The forms we see are its shadows. Our awareness, our ability to be consciously aware is born from this all-pervading consciousness. It is a microcosm of an even greater awareness that is immortal and the creator of all that we are.

Take a moment to look around you right now. What you're looking at is yourself. But you're not aware that these items, or those people, or this world is also you. This is because you're mind, just like your white blood cells, or your kidneys are incapable of being aware that they are apart of something greater. The ego, by nature, would never allow it.

Abandon the ego, its rules and kingdom, and there will no longer be a separation between this so called you and this so called world. The flesh no longer defines a border. And so when one loses themselves in meditation, one realizes that nothing separates their true identity from material such as cotton or pure light. We are the sky among the clouds. Our consciousness is there waiting for us to fly.

Text 3.43

बहिरकल्पिता वृत्तिः महाविदेहा ततः प्रकाशाअवरणक्षयः
bahir-akalpitā vṛttiḥ mahā-videhā tataḥ prakāśa-āvaraṇa-kṣayaḥ

bahiḥ	External
akalpitā	Unimaginable
vr̥tti	Thought wave
maha	Great
videhā	Out of body
tataḥ	Thence, by that
prakāśa	Light
āvaraṇa	Covering, veil
kṣayaḥ	Destruction

A great body-less one is when the formless state of mind eventually leaves the identity of the body. That is when the spiritual veil is destroyed.

Several years ago, bounty hunters had placed a $10,000 figure on my head if they could extract me from an endangered old growth redwood their employers were intent on logging. For three months, I meditated nearly ten stories up at the top of the tree without coming down once. My day consisted of ten hours meditation, two light meals (that braver revolutionaries would smuggle to me every couple of weeks), and the studying of the sutras of Hui-Neng. After the first three weeks, time became irrelevant. After the first month, I also became irrelevant. My body simply performed the motions of the creature who meditates and while the forest continued, I no longer did.

Eventually, I vaguely remembered having a specific body. The wind blew and I was there. The black bear scratched her nails at the bottom of the tree, and I was the sound. A hummingbird paused in front of my face for ages while I stared through her eyes at the strange looking hippie staring back at me. So long as I had no intention of existing as an *I*, what was left was the consciousness around that body, rather than just me, and my small mind experience of it. This is a state that occurs when what is left of this so called me is only light, and even that light is shed and left behind.

Text 3.44

स्थूलस्वरूपसूक्ष्मान्वयार्थवत्त्वसंयमात् भूतजयः
sthūla-svarūpa-sūkṣma-anvaya-arthavattva-saṁyamāt bhūtajayaḥ

sthūla	Gross
svarūpa	Own true form
sūkṣma	Subtle
anvaya	Constitution, sequence
arthavattva	An object's purpose
saṁyama	Concentration, meditation, and samadhi
bhūta	The five elements
jayaḥ	Victory, mastery

By practicing *saṁyama* on the architecture of an object [its gross attributes, nature, subtle attributes, constitution, and purpose], we master the elements.

Our thoughts alone are incapable of seeing truth. The mind works the same way any other bodily utility does; it seeks to self-preserve and grow. The mind is not conscious though. It is not aware of itself. It is just a utility. Your car is also a utility. But your car has no idea who you are. Like so, your mind has no idea who you are. It has no such ability.

What you are — is consciousness. Your awareness is just the very beginning of this truth. And from this awareness, all things come into form. The entire history of the world is reproduced in every fleeting moment. Where in the beginning, there is nothing. Only blissful emptiness. Then the moment you lose awareness, and try to hold on to some fleeting form — the world reveals itself in a cacophony of sensory experience.

At every moment, the material world and the mind appear simultaneously. Together they design the living moment. It begins with the mind requiring purpose or *arthavattva*. It perceives the material world out of need. This is why our first perception is a world that exists to serve us. The mind and world define the constitution or *anvaya* of these ego-serving objects. They use Occam's razor to cut and reveal only the *sūkṣma* or subtle influences that serve us best. They design their natures or *svarūpa*. And finally, they define the gross attributes or *sthūla* of these things.

For many people, they have no idea how pigeonholed their perception is based on the demands of their ego. This mind coupled with their material environment designs their very own personalized rat race. They could literally be in paradise, but living in hell. If we abide in awareness, we can observe this process of the mind holding hands with the material world attempting to design something fit for the ego. This sutra describes the architecture of material perception. Once we understand this system, we can leave this self behind.

Text 3.45

ततोऽणिमादिप्रादुर्भावः कायसंपत् तद्धरानभिघातश्च

tato-'ṇimādi-prādurbhāvaḥ kāyasaṁpat tad-dharānabhighātśca

tataḥ	Thence, by that
aṇiman	Mystic powers of weight, size, distance, etc.
prādurbhāvaḥ	Manifestation
kāya	The body
saṁpat	Perfection
tat	Whose, their
dharma	Nature, teaching, function
anabhighāta	Nonresistance
ca	And

So by *samyama*, all of these various powers manifest the perfect body with indestructible characteristics.

One of the greatest attainments of a spiritual seeker is dissolving the borders between themselves and the world. So when we say the words, I am — we are also implying the world around us. I am the beggar's hands, the wandering bird, and endless breeze. I am the crying child, the police siren, and broken leaf.

This is the perfected body of the yogi. When the body is the world itself. When the body is among every detail. When the body is all. You can not destroy this type of body. This body escapes even time itself.

The reason is because awareness doesn't depend on a living form. What we consider living is only a shadow of its truth. All of creation as we know it could be wiped clean from the surface of the Earth, but awareness will have never changed. Time will have never passed.

We are but mere waves among an infinite ocean. When we surrender this body to such an ocean — we watch the waves come and go, and the castles made of sand return to the sea.

Text 3.46

रूपलावण्यबलवज्रसंहननत्वानि कायसंपत्

rūpa-lāvaṇya-bala-vajra-saṁhananatvāni kāyasaṁpat

rūpa	Beauty of form
lāvaṇya	Charm, gracefulness
bala	Strength
vajra	Diamond
saṁhana-natvāni	Being of solid nature
kāya	The body
saṁpat	Perfection

This perfected body is also beautiful, graceful, energetic, and incapable of being broken.

When you surrender yourself, the world around you becomes you. The mountains become your hands. The rivers become your blood. The untold myriad of living beings become your eyes. The context of beauty and strength no longer describe something in particular. In that, without a body to perceive them, they no longer describe something that serves a particular body.

The mountains suddenly have no purpose. The rivers or cutting sunsets share no reason. And so when we describe them as beautiful — it's not because they serve us. It's because they reflect what is eternal, timeless, and indescribable. Like watching rain fall into the careless leaves of a forest; the strength and grace of the scene is in its directionless passage. This is the perfected body of the yogi.

Text 3.47

ग्रहणस्वरूपास्मिताअवयार्थवत्त्वसंयमातिन्द्रिय जयः

grahaṇa-svarūpa-asmitā-avaya-arthavattva-saṁyamāt-indriya jayaḥ

grahaṇa	Process of learning
svarūpa	Own nature, own essence
asmitā	The ego
anvaya	Inherent quality
arthavattva	Purposefulness
saṁyama	Concentration, meditation,
indriya	and samadhi
jayaḥ	Senses
	Mastery

Our perception is composed of knowledge, nature, ego, intellect, and consciousness. By performing samyama on perception, we understand this architecture and master the senses.

Our thoughts can only be shared among a few of us, but our awareness can be shared by all. This is is because awareness exists before things do, before thoughts, and well before even us. By dwelling in just awareness, we're dwelling in the origin of all things. It is from this pure awareness, we exist in what all of life has in common. A blissful place without reason because even reason hasn't occurred yet.

But most of us don't see this bliss because they are severely conditioned to feeling separated and unique. We have a title, a name, a career, a Facebook, a mirror, or even just a reflection in a lake. And all of these things encourage the idea of feeling separated. And then the want of being separated. To be something in particular.

Despite our ego's aspirations to be different, this isn't how consciousness works. Consciousness reflects itself through our perception. What we notice is both the same awareness we use to perceive it. It is the ego that begins the separation process. Which starts by assigning a purpose or *arthavattva*. When we see the trees, we are the trees. Except for many of us, one side of this reflection mistakenly believes it is something different. We mistakenly believe we are something different perceiving something separate. If we separate just a little more, we see the intellect recognizing an inherent quality called *anvaya*. A little further away, and we brandish Occam's razor to designate what serves this separate self best. We call this *asmitā*. Further away, we begin to smell, taste, see, touch, and hear this separation as nature or *svarupa*. The furthest we can possibly separate ourselves from awareness is in our knowledge of it. When we identify a name to a particular taste, or a thought to a particular image, a process called *grahaṇa*, we canonize our experience. We are at this point, fully separated from our awareness.

Lest we forget the path that led us to this separation, we can always find our way back. Back to the ocean we came from.

Text 3.48

ततो मनोजवित्वं विकरणभावः प्रधानजयश्च

tato mano-javitvaṁ vikaraṇa-bhāvaḥ pradhāna-jayaś-ca

tataḥ	Thence, by that
mano	Mind
javitvaṁ	Quickness
vikaraṇa	Tools [sense organs]
bhāvaḥ	Liberation, existence
pradhāna	Matter, nature
jaya	Victory
ca	And

From that mastered perception, everything moves at the speed of mind. It is independent of senses, and master over the cause of material.

For most of us, there is a latency between the present moment and our perception of it. But as we surrender this self — the latency stops existing. And life unfolds at the very speed in which our mind perceives it. But if there's a self, then there's a latency. And the ego uses this latency in perception to design what it wants to see.

The ego alongside the senses use Occam's razor to perceive only that which entertains us best. But the more we surrender this so called self, the more life has a chance to reveal itself as itself while it's happening. The more we surrender, the less there is difference between this so called me and this so called world.

In this state of mind, there is no duality. We no longer see the enemy and the friend; we see only the human. We no longer see life and death; we only see consciousness revealing itself.

In this state, we become masters of the material world. This is because we become fully aware that we're not of this world though among it. That our senses are only shadows of a deeper experience. And that life's motion is faster than our perception. And so we let go of our will to live — to live.

3.49

सत्त्वपुरुषान्यताख्यातिमात्रस्य
सर्वभावाअधिष्ठातृत्वं
सर्वज्ञातृत्वं च

sattva-puruṣa-anyatā-khyātimātrasya
sarva-bhāvā-adhiṣṭhātṛtvaṁ
sarva-jñātṛtvaṁ ca

sattva	Purity, light
puruṣa	True consciousness
anyata	Difference
khyāti	Discernment
mātra	Only
sarva	All
bhāva	State of existence, emotions
adhiṣṭhāṭṛtvaṁ	Supremacy over, mastery
sarva	All
jñātṛtva	State of knowledge
ca	And

Only the one who can tell the difference between consciousness and intellect has mastery and knowledge of everything.

They say at the top of the mountain, Lao Tzu left his shoes behind. At the other side of the river, the Buddha left his boat behind. At the doorway to enlightenment, nothing can come with you. You must abandon the religion that brought you there. You must give up your name, your soul, and all your pious ambitions. At the doorway of conscious awareness, nothing can come with you because everything, no matter how pure and meaningful it is — is still just a shadow of reality.

And so its extremely important to note that the last thread of connection; those shoes, that boat, or specifically the practice that will lead you to the summit is not the summit itself. Just as it is important to never mistake the forest for the path. If you want to see the forest, then appreciate what created the path. This is how we come to understand the forest. And we won't know the forest until the forest lives within us.

Text 3.50

तद्वैराग्यादपि दोषबीजक्षये कैवल्यम्
tad-vairāgyād-api doṣa-bīja-kṣaye kaivalyam

tad	That
vairāgyat	Nonattachment
api	Even
doṣa	Impurity, faults
bīja	Seed, root
kṣaye	Destruction
kaivalyam	Supreme independence

By abandoning mastery and knowledge, even destroying the seeds of all faults, supreme knowledge occurs.

The only thing standing in the way of presence is presence. In order to be present, we must let go of the concept of presence and the intention to be present. We must abandon our intention to be — so we can simply be.

We ask fearfully, but how will we know what do if we give up everything including our intention? Nature explains this one best. In that, once we give up trying to coerce the world, even if its for good intentions — nature will take care of itself. It knows exactly what to do. And will do so once we stop getting in the way.

Just take a gander at any abandoned home among the jungle. It won't be long before the flowering vines and music of the creatures breach its walls, and pull its beams back into the Earth it came from.

Text 3.51

स्थान्युपनिमन्त्रणे सङ्गस्मयाकरणं पुनरनिष्टप्रसङ्गात्

sthāny-upa-nimantraṇe saṅga-smaya-akaraṇaṁ punar-aniṣṭa-prasaṅgāt

sthāni	Celestial beings
upanimantraṇe	Upon the invitation
saṅga	Attachment
smaya	Smile
akaraṇaṁ	To avoid, refuse
punaḥ	Again
aniṣṭa	Undesirable
prasaṇgāt	Inclination toward

At the invitation of angels, don't allow yourself to become prideful, as you would be only renewing the undesirable connection with materialism, and samsaric living.

Physical health and a balanced state of mind are going to be obstacles to your practice. They might seem like a nice calling card to yoga, and in the first years of your practice, that might be the reason why you're practicing. But you will have only approached the first few steps of your soul so long as you still practice for some kind of material benefit.

Yoga is much deeper than this. Just as love is much more vast than this body. Just as love is much greater than just this life. Yoga like love doesn't involve an individual. These respective ideas, yoga and love are everything, everyone, and the spark of all motion and all action. Yoga will lead you to something greater than the self so long as your willing to practice for something greater than the self.

And so we must surrender who we are to what we are. And what we are, all of us, everything — the leaves brushing against the sidewalk, the traffic lights, the voice of a friend — is all boundless love. So when the angels invite us to play, this isn't a milestone of our achievement. There's nothing to be arrogant about because they've always been there waiting. Waiting for us to let go of the only thing that separates us, which is this world — in favor of love.

Text 3.52

क्षणतत्क्रमयोः संयमात् विवेकजंज्ञानम्
kṣaṇa-tat-kramayoḥ saṁyamāt vivekajaṁ-jñānam

kṣaṇa	Moment, instant
tat	Its [the moment]
kramayoḥ	Sequence
saṁyamāt	By saṁyama
viveka	Discernment
jam	Born of
jñānam	Knowledge

By samyama on the sequence of moments, knowledge is born from discrimination.

The past and future only exist in the obscure labyrinth of our imagination. In order to remember the past or see into the future, you must leave the present. In the still photograph of a falling leaf, evidence of a past and future are there. The leaf must have fallen from somewhere. It will eventually find the ground. But these are assumptions. They are not the picture.

We can't both see the past or future, and the photograph at the same time. The moment we drift away from presence, we exist in a world on to ourselves that we can't share with anyone. Our perception of what was or what will be is unreal. It will never exist for anyone outside of our very own obscure imagination.

Now here's the most important thing to note. Even when staring at the photograph, and pointing at the leaf, calling it a leaf, you are more than likely pointing to the past and not referring at all to what you're holding in your hand. Only by the deepest meditation, can one discriminate the sequence of past, present, and future, and see what is truly now.

Text 3.53

जातिलक्षणदेशैः अन्यताअनवच्छेदात् तुल्ययोः ततः प्रतिपत्तिः
jāti-lakṣaṇa-deśaiḥ anyatā-anavacchedāt tulyayoḥ tataḥ pratipattiḥ

jāti	Specie, category, type
lakṣaṇa	Distinguishing
deśa	characteristic
anyata	Place
anavacchedāt	Difference
tulyayoḥ	Not separated
tataḥ	Of two comparable objects
pratipattiḥ	Thereby, from that
	Precise understanding

This discrimination [3.52] leads one to distinguish two indistinguishable objects.

Human perception drags behind reality. Sometimes it crawls. We may have once seen a snake in the road, but now it's a tree branch. And because our perception is slower than reality, we see the snake until our consciousness can catch up.

But this sutra points at something even more subtle. Sometimes the object is, by all means, the same object. Like a friend who stands before us. They have not moved nor changed. But they are absolutely different than who and what they were just a moment ago.

The subtle drift of emotion, the velocity of thought, a bird passes the sun. Suddenly, your friend is enveloped in a memory and the memory speaks through your friend.

Who exactly is speaking to you? Is it your friend or the memory? Every object refracts consciousness. Like a television, the container may stay the same, but the programming is always changing. The content is not the object. Just like your thoughts are not you. Their thoughts are not them.

We're just mirrors reflecting thousands of years of emotional history in the form of symbols, words, and ideas. Whether it's someone speaking or someone perceiving --

both of these actions conduct our ancient emotional history. And while performing either, we transform into the content and lose sight of the vessel. We forget we're watching the movie.

But the yogi observes this happening. They can see the difference among the seemingly changeless.

Text 3.54

तारकं सर्वविषयं सर्वथाविषयमक्रमंचेति विवेकजं ज्ञानम्
tārakaṁ sarva-viṣayaṁ sarvathā-viṣayam-akramaṁ-ceti vivekajaṁ jñānam

tārakam	One who transcends,
sarva	liberates
viṣayam	All
sarvathā	Object
akramam	Everywhere, all beings, all
ca	time
iti	Non-sequential
viveka	And
jam	Thus
jñānam	Discernment
	Born [of discernment]
	Knowledge

Knowledge born of this kind of discrimination [3.52 - 3.53], is the liberator; it is available everywhere in everything without sequence.

There is an important difference between high knowledge or *jñānam* and knowledge. Knowledge is composed of structured ideas curated by practice and objective criticism. High knowledge is already complete without parts. It has no structure nor authors. It is a channel of wisdom available without dialect or reason.

Love is the best example of high knowledge. This high knowledge is available anytime we surrender our intellect for the sake of love. It is called the great liberator because love without reason is the most encompassing context to life. It doesn't survive on the welfare of our fleeting wants and desires. Instead, it exists without reason and therefore it is as immortal as rain.

The medium of selfless service, is in itself, its own reward. Why is that? Because in the act of love, instead of being a short-lived human being in a fragile body — you become the immortal body of the entire universe acting through a human being. The context is all encompassing. At the top of such a mountain, the heart can only reach for love. It can only be love. And you can only see love in every circumstance. This is high knowledge.

Text 3.55

सत्त्वपुरुषयोः शुद्धिसाम्ये कैवल्यम्
sattva-puruṣayoḥ śuddhisāmye kaivalyam

sattva	Pure quality
puruṣayoh	Of the true consciousness
śuddhi	Purity
sāmye	Upon sameness
kaivalyam	Absolute independence

When your awareness is as pure as pure consciousness, this is absolute liberation.

One of the most common mistakes seekers make is imitating purity. They follow all the motions of liberated beings while still interacting in a framework of fight or flight. To find original purity, to locate your deepest sense of love, you must simply observe the breath. And use the breath as a litmus test against your currents of thought, your emotional reactions and attention.

Eventually, a majority of your conscious thought will subside, and you will be able to navigate your subtle subconsciousness. Your almost forgotten histories, old traumas, core memories. Knowing them gives you your own personalized architecture of how and why you act the way you do.

Which leads you even deeper to your unconsciousness, the fundamental seeds of your ego. A place without dialogue. Where the origin of emotion rests waiting for the light to spawn. And if you interact here long enough, you will make peace with it. They will no longer spawn. And you'll find the deepest state. Which is a state beyond states. The origin of time and space. Where all things manifest from.

This place is no different than God. No different than Truth. And you will carry the context of this state of mind with you all the way back to your superficial conscious state. The one you started with. The passing trucks, a newspaper blowing in the wind, a dog barking from a distance — will be no different than the place you came from. No different than God. No different than Truth. Absolute liberation.

Chapter Four

Text 4.1

जन्मओषधिमन्त्रतपस्समाधिजाः सिद्धयः
janma-oṣadhi-mantra-tapas-samādhi-jāḥ siddhayaḥ

janma	Birth
oṣadhim	Medicine, herbs, drugs
mantra	Sacred chant
tapaḥ	Austerity, sacrefice
samādhi	Meditative absorption,
jāḥ	enlightenment
siddhayaḥ	Born, arise
	Supernatural powers

Higher consciousness can be found by birth, drugs, mantra, selflessness, or yoga.

Some of us are born with a taste for higher consciousness. Since birth, they've preferred intention over action; simplicity more than sensationalism, love instead of competition.

Others have been exposed to a broader sense of awareness through the use of psychedelic and psychoactive drugs. Substances that disconnect, alter, or extend your peripheral consciousness to re-examine the authenticity of your supposed identity and your relationship with the world.

Some take up a sacred word, a name for God, or just a sound, and dedicate themselves so feverishly to it, that the sound becomes the context of their consciousness. These mantras can become so persistent that unlike rational thought, they can follow you into your sleep, deep into your unconscious perception, and be a thread to help you navigate your way through the labyrinth of awareness no matter what state of mind or situation you are in.

Selflessness means effortlessness. And effortlessness means without ego. Those who act without ego, who just follow the orders of their teachers without any interest in anything in return — gain insight on the mechanical workings of the consciousness. This is because when you stop serving the self, you realize how little you ever had to do with such a self. By serving the world, you quickly discover that entire personality we wrap around this supposed me was never us.

Lastly, there is yoga. Yoga, as outlined in the Yoga Sutras, lead us to the state of samadhi. Samadhi is the result of absolute absorption in our origin.

The consciousness is like any other muscle. When it's weak, we cry at our broken phone. When it's strong, we notice a flower blooming through a concrete sidewalk. These are just five examples of how we can expand and develop conscious awareness.

Text 4.2

जात्यन्तरपरिणामः प्रकृत्यापूरात्

jāty-antara-pariṇāmaḥ prakṛty-āpūrāt

jātī	Birth, form of existence
antara	Inner
pariṇāmaḥ	Transition, evolution
prakr̥tyā	Material nature
āpūrāt	By filling, completion

As material nature changes, we take birth by pouring into new forms.

Intentions pour through us like wandering clouds. They take birth in us, shapeshifting into the things we say, the things we build. Intentions pour like water into the vehicles that serve them best.

Perhaps it began with something we said. Then it's a written word. A flower. A passing bee. Laughter. A child being born. On a seemingly simple walk among the woods, you can observe the inertia of millions of years of survival, trauma, love, and loyalty whispering through your thoughts and subtle movements.

Emotions possess you. They take birth in you and you help them pass on. The intellect can help you observe these emotional passages instead of being possessed by them.

If the intellect serves you best, it will acknowledge that you are not these movements nor this vehicle we call the body. From the vantage point of the higher consciousness, we observe nature taking birth into all of its various forms. Like water, pouring into new life, new design, new ideas — each stream from thousands of years away, filling in the gaps.

Text 4.3

निमित्तमप्रयोजकं प्रकृतीनांवरणभेदस्तु ततः क्षेत्रिकवत्
nimittam-aprayojakaṁ prakr̥tīnāṁ-varaṇa-bhedastu tataḥ kṣetrikavat

nimitta	Instrumental cause
aprayojakaṁ	Non-causal, nonrelevant
prakr̥ti	Material nature
varaṇa	Wall around a rice field
bheda	Piercing
tu	But
tataḥ	Thence, by that
kṣetrikavat	Like a farmer

The cause of creation is not the individual who moves it. They are, like the farmer, just piercing the protective covering of the origin.

When things happen to us, our intellect can direct our reaction. We have the right to choose. But whose intellect is this? Intellect, just like our interests and fears is also just another evolving, transient attribute.

Intellect has passed through countless evolutions before taking birth in this body. And we all share a part in this evolution. But intellect can only shapes the world. It wasn't the world's cause. As Patanjali explains, intellect can only, at best, pierce the illusive coverings of nature allowing it to flow more freely. Remove the buildings, and you can see nature. Remove the ego, and you see others. Remove every superfluous habit you have, and you will find what really makes you happy.

Intellect can help impact the flow of nature. But it's important to note that the root of this nature is not intellect. It's root is far deeper than the ability to discriminate.

Text 4.4

निर्माणचित्तान्यस्मितामात्रात्
nirmāṇa-cittāny-asmitā-mātrāt

nirmāṇa	Created
cittāni	Minds
asmitāḥ	Ego
mātrāt	Alone

Minds are created only from ego.

No thought is ever original. The mind is just a vehicle that carries. Thoughts pass like leaves among a breeze. Some stick. Others don't. It is pure coincidence. And so from birth, we carefully design our personal architectures of thought by whatever ideas happen to find their way into our lives. Before this ego takes root, we share the same instincts to love and survive. By these instincts, no living being is different. And from this root, we catch wind of ideas, and forage what best serves those instincts.

But ideas are superfluous. Ideas come and go. Thoughts decay. People decay. Entire civilizations decay. But the instinct to love is eternal. The entire material world is an echo of this. So treat your mind the same way you treat a falling leaf. It will not last. Why save this one leaf, when the whole world needs it to return to the soil? Your beliefs will outlive you by a few generations. But your will to love will never be forgotten. The mind is a coincidence, but you, my friend — are not.

Text 4.5

प्रवृत्तिभेदे प्रयोजकं चित्तमेकमनेकेषाम्

pravr̥tti-bhede prayojakaṁ cittam-ekam-anekeṣām

pravr̥tti	Manifestation
bhede	Difference
prayojakam	The cause
cittam	Mind
ekam	One
anekeṣām	Of many

One mind among many directs their different activities.

Ideas are magnetic. We're drawn to them. If a person is a source of new thought, we imitate them. If a culture is the source of new ideas, we follow it. New ideas create fresher perspective, and a new perspective is like opening a window in our mind to let the light in.

We crave that light. Our personality survives off of that light. The fresher and cleaner the ideas, the more relevant life becomes. And so we're attracted to creativity because it replenishes us. And we drink this nectar by mimicking its source.

What many of us are not aware of, is that these sources originate in a patient zero. A single teacher. Or a few but not many. And all of our actions, are merely echoes of their work. In this way, even if you have not met your guru, you're already receiving instructions from them. And to find your guru, you simply follow your intentions back to their source.

Text 4.6

निर्माणचित्तान्यस्मितामात्रात्

tatra dhyānajam-anāśayam

tatra	Of these [enlightened ones]
dhyānajam	Born from meditation
aśaya	Lasting impression
anāśayam	Without influence

Of these five types of conscious expansion [birth, drugs, mantra, austerities, or yoga], meditation is the only one free of karma.

There's many ways to demonstrate conscious awareness. Some people use it to create powerful religions, powerful corporations. Some manifest influential arts and sciences, or even run for political office. All of these products are available to us; be it by birth, drugs, mantra, service, or samadhi. But meditation is the only sustainable form of conscious expansion.

Being born into fortunate circumstances does not guarantee you fortune for life. Taking drugs to find new awareness isn't sustainable. Mantra, performing good deeds, and yoga without meditation is at best — just sensational. Why does meditation separate itself from these actions? Because meditation is the act of losing oneself absolutely.

No ego. No effort. That is meditation.

So to guarantee the growth of your awareness, you must position the self to be selfless. Everything else on the market being sold as spiritual, or charity, or yogic, or self-help are materialistic and unreal. None of these will finish the job. Only you can help yourself by giving up the self.

Text 4.7

कर्माशुक्लाकृष्णं योगिनः त्रिविधमितरेषाम्
karma-aśukla-akṛṣṇaṁ yoginaḥ trividham-itareṣām

karmā	Physics, cause and effect
aśuklā	Not white
a-kṛṣnam	Not black
yoginaḥ	Of the yogi
tri	Three
tri-vidham	Three fold
itareṣām	Of the others

The yogi's actions are not simply black and white. They are a shade of grey for all.

Every action is veined by a thousand intentions. Every subtle movement, a drop of water, a dog barking in the distance — each action is threaded with a history you will never know, from ages you have never lived through.

Despite our best intions, no action is perfect. Every meal is at the cost of others. Every temple was built on the destruction of the nature it supposedly serves. But outside of what is fortunate for some and wretched for others, is a space that exists between.

It is called an eternal space. A space that is eternally quiet. Even in the middle of a traffic jam of emotion, injustice, and pain, there is always available — a presence of silence.

Not because there's no noise. It's a silence because there's no ego or listener. Just presence. And that silence is Truth.

Every one our actions deny this truth because they imply a doer, a me, or an I am doing this. And because there is an I, there is karma. And that karma will inevitably help some and hurt others. And so while there is a me, there is no quiet. There is no peace. But if you act on behalf of the space between, there is no karma. No shades of black or white. Only peace.

Text 4.8

ततः तद्विपाकानुगुणानामेवाभिव्यक्तिः वासनानाम्

tataḥ tad-vipāka-anugṇānām-eva-abhivyaktiḥ vāsanānām

tataḥ	From this
tad	Whose, those
vipāka	Results, fruits
tad-vipāka	Ripen
anuguṇānam	Based on the three qualities
eva	Only
abhi	To
vyakti	Manifestation
abhi-vyaktiḥ	To manifest
vāsanām	Fragrance, subliminal impression

We become perfumed by all of these actions.

Trauma leaves an imprint on our psyche that could take decades, if not lifetimes, to overcome. Vice versa, so does love, or any varying degree of phenomenon in between.

In Sanskrit, conscious imprints come in two forms, *vāsanām* and *samskaram* which Patanjali separately defines in this and the following verse. This verse discusses *vāsanām* which translates to fragrance or that which dwells.

Meaning, the influence is there, dwelling around us like a perfume, but doesn't mean it's written into us yet. And therefore, we still reserve the rights and means to not allow these things to become us. The following verse, we discover *samskara* which are the grooves written into our vinyl thought patterns.

Text 4.9

जाति देश काल व्यवहितानामप्यान्तर्यां स्मृतिसंस्कारयोः एकरूपत्वात्
jāti deśa kāla vyavahitānām-apy-āntaryāṁ smṛti-saṁskārayoḥ ekarūpatvāt

jāti	Birth, class, caste
deśa	Place
kāla	Time
vyavahitānām	Seperated
api	Even
anantaryaṁ	Uninterrupted sequence
smṛti	Memory
saṁskārayoḥ	Subliminal impressions
eka	One
rūpa	Form, being

Memory and instinct [saṁskārayoḥ] are identical even though they might be born from different time and places.

Millions of years of strategic competition designed our vertebrae. We are another mind among a mala of evolutionary choices. And so just possessing a body part such as the vertebrae, we adopt with it its instinctual consciousness. We inherit not just the function of the body part, but the consciousness of the one that needed it.

Sometimes the body part will evolve and cause the consciousness to follow, and sometimes the consciousness will evolve and cause the body to follow. We can observe this back and forth over the course of many millennia, but we can also observe this back and forth in our simple day to day as well.

If the vertebrae is constricted by inflexibility or dystrophy, then our mindset reflects it. If this carries on for several generations, we begin evolving to physically compensate the lifestyle that vertebrae requires. To understand *saṁskāra*, our written conscious patterns, we now have accept that every single bone, muscle, tissue, cognitive function of the brain, and body system carry their own hand-written consciousness that blends together in a chaotic whirlpool of this -- I am.

Some patterns stem from millions of years ago, but they are no different than our recent day to day habits like the cravings for tea, or our fascination with creativity.

Text 4.10

तासामनादित्वं चाशिषो नित्यत्वात्
tāsām-anāditvaṁ cāśiṣo nityatvāt

tāsām	Of them [saṁskāra]
anāditvaṁ	No beginning
ca	And
āśiṣaḥ	Desire, will to live
nityatvāt	Eternal, without end

Our patterns have no beginning because the will to live is eternal.

Life is a domino effect with no beginning. You can trace every action back to some kind of source, but never an origin. Instead, all we witness is patterns creating patterns.

Enlightenment isn't discovered by perfecting these patterns. Nor is it discovered by creating better patterns. People who invest their lives in perfecting good habits and holy rituals are wasting their time. Good habits are not the goal. They are a side effect.

If you just practice good habits, you can still be an asshole. But if you dwell in pure awareness, good habits are inevitable. There is no such thing as a perfect pattern, or a perfect religion, or a perfect practice. But there is a perfect awareness. Because when awareness has no ego, it has no pattern. It has no time, no past nor future, and no beholder.

There is no one person responsible for being aware. And when this presence is held, patterns fall apart. Addictions decay. Habits fade. And suddenly, the people and the environment around us can be seen as they are.

And so while the yogi commits themselves to patterns like non-violence, cleanliness, and truth — they should see these things as side effects, not goals. Vegetarianism is a side-effect of being aware, not an ends. Quitting smoking is a side effect of being aware, not counting cigarettes. Patterns like life will go on indefinitely, but you are not these things.

Text 4.11

हेतुफलाश्रयालम्बनैःसंगृहीतत्वातेषामभावेतदभावः
hetu-phala-āśraya-ālambanaiḥ-saṁgr̥hītatvāt-eṣām-abhāve-tad-abhāvaḥ

hetu	Cause
phala	Fruit, effect
āśraya	Based upon
ālambanaiḥ	Support
saṁgr̥hītatvāt	Being held together
eṣām	Of them
abhāve	In the absence
tad	Of them
abhāvaḥ	Disappear, unmanifest

Since patterns are composed of cause, intention, substratum, and an object — when these disappear, so do the patterns.

Uncertainty is extremely uncomfortable. Having never found a comfort in not knowing, we strive to know by identifying everything around us — even if we have to make it up.

This is the driving force behind our materialism. Because taking possession of the world around us, allows us to have an understanding (even if we have to make up all the facts).

The very first and most valued possession we make up is the self. At birth, our intention is to survive. We don't see the world through the eyes of others. We don't realize how simple it is to share consciousness. We don't realize how unoriginal we are. And so we think, I must be different. My flesh must be a border between the world and the I am. The forests, the trees, the animals at night must be something separate.

And from this starting point, we design the entire context of our lives around what serves this separation from the world. It's a separation between love and lover. A separation between you and your higher self. And a separation between you and God.

This is how our patterned habits thrive. Our programmed conscious patterns can only survive from the illusion of separation. But if you abandon the self you become the world, patterns fall apart. Become the world, and there are no longer habits that drive you. Realize that nothing separates this so called world and this so called self, and you will stumble upon reality.

Text 4.12

अतीतानागतं स्वरूपतोऽस्तिअध्वभेदाद् धर्माणाम्
atīta-anāgataṁ svarūpato-'sti-adhvabhedād dharmāṇām

atīta	Past
anāgataṁ	Future
svarūpataḥ	Its own form
asti	There is, remain
adhva	Path
bhedāt	Because of variance
adhvabhedāt	Because of varied paths
dharmāṇāṁ	Of the inherent characteristics

The past and future exist because things change.

It's a common misconception to think that time is linear. We think, time must have passed when my finger touched the flame because now it's burnt. That something starts at 0 and ends somewhere else. But time is more irrational than this. Because the past hides in our presence. And we decorate our perception with the future. Presence is what's left.

The consciousness makes a cocktail of all three [past, present, and future] and composes a designer moment. It can be very confusing to perceive what is actually now, and not what's just a memory or imagination. So to have an accurate context of time, we have to acknowledge it from a place of pure presence. From a place of virgin awareness untouched by opinion. A place before the ego found a home called me.

It is there you'll be able to see that countless generations of people who burned the same finger. They made the same mistake. And people just like you, in the same place will continue to do it eternally. Suddenly, you realize that before you touched the flame, you were already burned. The burning never started, and it will never stop. What you believe has just become, has already been and will be forever. And so it goes.

Text 4.13

ते व्यक्तसूक्ष्माः गुणात्मानः
te vyakta-sūkṣmāḥ guṇa-atmānaḥ

te	They [past, present, future]
vyakta	Manifest
sūkṣmāḥ	Subtle
guṇa	Of three basic elements
atmānaḥ	The absolute, supersoul

These characteristics [past, present, future] are composed of the qualities; rajas, tamas, and sattvas.

Our patchwork perception is composed out of memory, presence, and imagination. And each of these shades of illusion are colored by three qualities; rajas, tamas, and sattvas. Rajas is energy, movement, excitement. Tamas is lethargy and pause. Sattvas is light, realization, or truth.

If you eat rajasic foods [espresso, peppers, sugar] you become excited. If you eat tamasic foods [oil, butter, bread] you become tired. And if you eat sattvas foods [salads, lentils, veggies] you become level-minded.

But these three qualities also exist in all aspects of reality, and we consume them through experience. We are what we eat. At every given moment, those three qualities design the events and world around you based on the world that came before them. In reality, we are not actors of actions, but merely vehicles for these three qualities to pass through by their own inertia.

There is an ink meant for life composed of these three qualities. And we use that ink to paint the past, present, and future all occurring at once — in the present moment.

Text 4.14

परिणामैकत्वात् वस्तुतत्त्वम्

pariṇāma-ikatvāt vastu-tattvam

pariṇāma	Change
ekatvāt	Singleness, unique
vastu	Object, thing
tattvam	Thatness, reality

Everything is composed by change.

In a classical Western thought, we define the world with dualities. Your health is either good or bad. Big or small. Yes or no. But in Hinduism, there is a third quality. We refer to this third quality as a transcendental quality, or the quality of reality.

So instead of just being either healthy or sick, we also determine the reality of that health. A saddhu may appear physically famished, but emotionally stable-minded and peaceful. Instead of judging whether he is heathy or sick, we also include what is the context of his health? How sober is his experience of health?

You could be eating well, looking great, doing great things, but have no context whatsoever of reality or the people around you. Is that still healthy? So health is not one over the other, but a blend of all three that works best. These three qualities compose your relationships, habits, intentions, friends, and ultimately, your state of mind. And these qualities are in constant movement, constant change.

Much like atoms are rapidly rearranging even in the most sedentary objects such as a stone or a broken branch. Our consciousness shepherds these three qualities around us. The consciousness composes the body it possesses and the world around itself. An unrealized consciousness will perpetuate whatever coincidental circumstances it falls under. But a realized soul will be in a constant state of tailoring the world around it towards reality regardless of its duality.

Text 4.15

वस्तुसाम्ये चित्तभेदात्तयोर्विभक्तः पन्थाः
vastusāmye citta-bhedāt-tayorvibhaktaḥ panthāḥ

vastu	Object, thing
sāmye	Sameness
citta	Mind
bhedāt	Because of difference
tayoḥ	Whose
vibhaktaḥ	Different
panthāḥ	Traveler, paths

The same thing perceived by different minds will have different appearances.

We all see something unique. No sky is the same color blue. No flower will ever appear the same.

We inherit our perception, and then our perception is left behind when we die. Our life is but one mala among generations of kaleidoscopic filters. Each filter is an individual's life pitch bending the reality it inherits and passing it on to those it influenced.

We see and we reciprocate our sight on to the world. Eventually the world becomes what we thought it was. But never, necessarily, what it actually is.

Text 4.16

न चैकचित्ततन्त्रं चेद्वस्तु तदप्रमाणकं तदा किं स्यात्

na caika-citta-tantraṁ cedvastu tad-apramāṇakaṁ tadā kiṁ syāt

na	Not
ca	And
eka	One
citta	Mind
tantram	Dependent
cet	If
vastu	Object, thing
tat	That
apramāṇakaṁ	Not recognized
tadā	Then
kim	What
syāt	Happens

The world is not dependent on our perception. What happens to an object when it isn't perceived?

There's an enormous difference between perceiving something in particular and perceiving awareness. Perception is illusion. Perception depends on limited physical abilities, limited senses, and our Occam's razor of preference. Even the most clearest experience in life is going to be a watered down version of what life really is.

This is why, if we don't perceive something, then in our absence — it never existed. Because perception is so imaginative that the world itself can only exist because of it.

Awareness, however, is different from perception. Awareness is an experience without dialogue. Awareness exists before it comes into contact with a body that senses. It isn't dependent on the senses nor on the perceiver. And so it is beyond description. If you remove the being who experiences this awareness, the awareness is still there. The world is still there.

Perception is indeed born from awareness. Just as illusion is born from awareness. But awareness — awareness is unborn. Awareness has yet to be born. And when it is, it becomes perception which is immediately illusion and false. This is why the act of dwelling in awareness means dwelling in our origin. We are essentially swimming upstream to the fountainhead of awareness. A place before the world came into being.

Text 4.17

तदुपरागापेक्षित्वात् चित्तस्य वस्तुज्ञाताज्ञातं
tad-uparāga-apekṣitvāt cittasya vastu-jñātājñātaṁ

tad	It [the mind]
uparāga	Colored by
apekṣitvāt	Depending on
cittasya	Of the mind
vastu	Thing, object
jñātājñātaṁ	What is known and not known

A thing is known or not known based on the mind's disposition.

The further you distance your perception from awareness, the more the world begins to take shape. It takes ideas, and memories, and emotional connections that interweave and blind you from even seeing the world you're surrounded by.

Eventually it takes you. And so even though we might be surrounded by the same things. You will only notice the things in particular that serve your path. Even the color of the sky will be of a different hue.

Text 4.18

सदाज्ञाताः चित्तवृत्तयः तत्प्रभोः पुरुषस्यापरिणामित्वात्
sadājñātāḥ citta-vrttayaḥ tat-prabhoḥ puruṣasya-
apariṇāmitvāt

sadā	Always
jñātāḥ	Are known
citta	Mind
vṛttayaḥ	Thought waves
tat-prabhoḥ	From one's master
puruṣasya	Of the puruṣa
apariṇāmitvāt	Because of not changing

The changes in the mind can always be recognized by the changeless pure awareness.

In a state of pure awareness, the senses are no longer available. The ego has yet to be born. This is the fountainhead of experience. From here, all things come into existence. Because it is the source of all reality, nothing can affect it. This is why we call this awareness changeless" and eternal.

From it, the world comes into being. First there was light. Then form. Then life. Then our perception of life. And the myriad of details as infinite as the stars.

Everything is in constant change. So to have a sober perspective of it all, we have to understand everything's source — which is absolute awareness. The closer we posture ourselves to this absolute awareness, the better the vantage point we can have to observe the changing landscape.

In yoga, we carry the breath like a periscope to see beyond the confines of our limited perception. The breath can observe what the senses can't. If we lose focus of the breath, then in a greater sense, we've lost touch with the world around us. Once again, we become mired in the fantasy land of our imagination.

To the Zen Buddhists, this is considered death. And when we find the breath again, we are born again. Born into the present moment. What is left of us is both available and speechless. And so we follow the breath to awareness. And from awareness, we can watch the world rise and fall — eternally.

Text 4.19

न तत्स्वाभासं दृश्यत्वात्
na tat-svābhāsaṁ dṛśyatvāt

na	Not
tat	Whose
svā	Itself
bhāsam	Illuminating
svābhāsam	Self illuminating
dṛśyatvāt	Perceptibility

Nor is the mind self-illuminating because it is the after-effect of illumination.

First, there is awareness. Then there is mind. If we step away from awareness, a mind can take shape. And so we shouldn't look at the mind as a means of finding awareness. The mind is its biproduct. We can only gather clues about the machine the product was made from, but not the machine itself.

What is awareness if we can't use the mind to understand it? Awareness is beyond object, beyond mind, beyond the act of mindfulness. In yoga asana, we teach this concept by practicing *drstis*, or points of focus [stare at the hands, stare at the toes..] during our asana practice. These are not specific points of focus, but endless eternal directions you are to lose the self in. And to keep losing the self. Like a violinist loses the self in the music. Or how a fish can lose the self and become the ocean.

Or how a zen monks is instructed to keep looking despite assuming she's already found it. The idea is to break the rotary mind and its black and white assumptions. We may not be able to see beyond the mind, but at least we can observe its very real border. From here, we envision something further. Something beyond the realm of our individualized perception. We find a self without borders or context.

Once the self has no context, the movements of our body, our words, and inspiration coalesce in unison with a far greater consciousness. An awareness beyond the mind's imagination.

Text 4.20

एक समये चोभयानवधारणम्
eka samaye c-obhaya-an-avadhāraṇam

eka	One
samaye	Time
eka-samaye	Simultaneously
ca	And
ubhaya	Both
anavadhāraṇaṁ	Non discernment

The mind and the object of the mind's focus can not be understood at the same time.

Both the self and the present moment can't exist at the same time. You have to choose. And you have to make this choice in every waking moment; ego or presence, me or truth.

This can be an extremely difficult concept to understand. As discussed in previous sutras, the ego is in everything. Even in the act of conscious awareness. Because even the attempt of seeing the world truthfully is likely just the ego doing its usual thing but under the banner of enlightenment.

So to help pierce through the ego, we must examine its origin. The ego comes from the same fountainhead that all of reality does. This fountainhead is wordless, meaningless, and beyond reason. It is the source of all creation. When we distance ourselves from this fountainhead, we find pattern, definition, subject and object.

If you stand far enough away from that origin, you will eventually find a self, and a strange belief that you are somehow something separate and unique.

But the self is not this body. The real self isn't this short-lived life or this fleeting personality. The real self, who you truly are — is the fountainhead. And at its source, you are unborn. And as your attention falls away from this origin, you become the trees, the birds overhead, and the myriad of beings that populate the psychic universe.

Don't be distracted by these fleeting thoughts, or the vessel that carries them. You will never be able to entertain ideas of realization and be realized at the same time. The Zen master hangs on a branch from their mouth. Speak one word and they falls. And so to experience enlightenment, you have to abandon the realization of enlightenment.

Text 4.21

चित्तान्तर दृश्ये बुद्धिबुद्धेः अतिप्रसङ्गः स्मृतिसंकरश्च
cittāntara dṛśye buddhi-buddheḥ atiprasaṅgaḥ smṛti-saṁkaraś-ca

citta	Mind
āntara	Other
dṛśye	Seen by
buddhi	Intellect
buddheḥ	Perception
buddhi-buddheḥ	Perceiver of intellect
atiprasaṅgaḥ	Superficiality, unwarranted
smṛti	connection
saṁkaraḥ	Memory
ca	Mixture, confusion
	And

If you could see through someone else's mind, there would be infinite feedback. Memory would become perpetually confused.

The mind works just like a reflective orb. Place it amongst the world, and it will distort the color and light around it. You can say the contents are distorted. But only because the very medium of the orb is distorted. It doesn't matter what shape or size the orb is. Any version of the orb is always going to, in some way, distort the world it's enveloped by.

We must accept that truth exists outside of the mind's perspective. And if we depend on another mind to see truth, we're only abstracting with our mind an abstraction of someone else's mind.

When we emulate someone's perfection, or their happiness, it would be like listening to the feedback between two radios. There's nothing to find there. Instead of listening to the teacher, observe what the teacher is listening to.

Text 4.22

चितेरप्रतिसंक्रमायाः
तदाकारापत्तौ स्वबुद्धि संवेदनम्
citer-aprati-saṁkramāyāḥ
tad-ākāra-āpattau svabuddhi saṁ-vedanam

citeḥ	Of the mind
aprati	Not
saṁkramāyāḥ	Moving around
tad	That [mind]
ākāra	Form
apattau	Pervading
sva	Its own, reflexive
buddhi	Intellect
svabuddhi	Self knowledge
saṁ	Fully, completely
vedanam	Knowledge

[Enlightenment follows when] the consciousness remains unchanged as it manifests into the many forms it is surrounded by.

Imagine the consciousness as an infinite ocean. An ocean rife with wandering creatures. They emanate from, exist by, and return to the ocean they were born from. Creatures just like our endless thoughts and manifested forms. When observed as a whole, the greater living being is the ocean itself. The creatures come and go, but the ocean remains the same.

Our consciousness pours into the world around us causing an ebb and flow of strangers, lovers, and glittering memories. Just like the ocean, these things come and go, but the greater life is the body they emanate from.

If you observe an ocean's life — the evolution of its inhabitants, their conquest for tomorrow — you acquire a greater understanding of how the ocean as a whole thinks. Just as the greater whole that you're apart of thinks. A greater whole that whispers to you when you're quiet enough to listen. Whispers that can be followed back to an origin. Follow them far enough, and you will find an ocean. And from there, you can think as the ocean.

And as you watch the myriad of creatures evolve, and crawl out of the water, discover the invention of flight, society and war — the context of each story becomes just a fleeting ripple among a greater calm.

And so to understand this sutra, we must accept the limitations of the consciousness. We may never be able to perceive the world as itself, but we can, at the very least, surrender the urge to stand in the way of the one that sees.

Text 4.23

द्रष्टृदृश्योपरक्तं चित्तं सर्वार्थम्
draṣṭṛ-dṛśy-opa-raktaṁ cittaṁ sarva-artham

draṣṭṛ	The seer
dṛśya	That which is seen
ūpa	From close up
raktam	To color
cittam	Mind
sarva	All
artham	Goal

Everything in life is manifested by some coloring of the seer and the seen.

The same breeze of uncertainty and imagination passes through our dreams as it does our waking life. There are no boundaries to fantasy. Who we are and what we see can be anything at all. The mind is limitless.

What then, pray tell, does the seeker focus on? Enlightenment? That's a dream. Truth? Another dream. Peace? An illusion. Any idea is as useless as a compass in outer space. There is no gravity. No context. So what then is left?

Sometimes, the easiest way to wake up from a dream — is to realize you're dreaming.

Text 4.24

तदसङ्ख्येय वासनाभिः चित्रमपि परार्थम् संहत्यकारित्वात्

tad-asaṅkhyeya vāsanābhiḥ citram-api parārtham saṁhatya-kāritvāt

tad	That
asaṅkhyeya	Uncountable
vāsanābhiḥ	Fragrance, subliminal
citram	impressions
api	Varied
para	Also
artham	Other
saṁhatya	Goal, purpose
kāritāt	Union, connection
	Because of acting

This limitless mind exists by extension of a greater consciousness that uses it to interact with the world.

When you blur the distance between every individual life — you see the story of an even greater being that acts through every life. A greater being whose body is composed of its countless creatures. Creatures that evolved from single cells to beings that could climb from out of the ocean, grow wings, and grace the sky. Beings that could register color, sonar, scent, music, and radio. For every new adaptation of consciousness, life tiptoed closer to realizing itself. The entirety of our life is just one small movement in this process. We are the universe realizing itself.

Text 4.25

विशेषदर्शिनः आत्मभावभावनानिवृत्तिः
viśeṣa-darśinaḥ ātmabhāva-bhāvanā-nivṛttiḥ

viśeṣa	Distinction
darśinaḥ	The seer
ātma	The true self, supersoul
bhāva	Nature
ātmabhāva	Soul of nature
bhāvanā	Meditation, development towards
nivṛttiḥ	Cessation

When you discover the difference between the *I am* that sees and our greater soul — our personal nature and our meditation vanish.

Until we are ourselves, everything is fight or flight. Constantly running, constantly fighting. Rarely, if ever, do we pause and appreciate the world without wanting something from it.

Only the luckiest of us have ever tiptoed after rumors of something greater than this fight or flight. Something more fulfilling, more encompassing. That experience is only available in our resignation.

If we resign ourselves enough, we eventually realize that the entirety of our life is just one small mala in a chain of lives being chanted on by something far greater than us.

From this perspective, things like happiness and fear are completely different. Because we realize that things don't have to serve us for us to be happy. Instead, we are comforted by the world simply being itself — whatever that may be. Little by little, our personal habits, fears, and anxieties crumble and vanish. Our meditation and our attempt to meditate vanish. We become the living expression of our origin — our fountainhead — our yoga.

Text 4.26

तदा विवेकनिम्नं कैवल्यप्राग्भारं चित्तम्
tadā viveka-nimnaṁ kaivalya-prāg-bhāraṁ cittam

tadā	Then
viveka	Discernment
nimnam	Inclined towards
kaivalya	Pure liberation
prāg-bhāraṁ	Inclined toward
cittam	Of the mind

Differentiate the mind and the soul, and everything will lead to liberation.

It was our ego that chose this path, this path of enlightenment™. Our ego looked at enlightenment and decided this was its path to power. And so it carefully observed the most superficial and fantastic representations of enlightenment.

Beginners to the path cling to the obvious; a calm voice, enormous golden altars, grandiose suffering. They evangelize their beliefs so their ego can wear their beliefs.

But enlightenment is a trap. I say this because it's actually suicide. The ego doesn't realize this at first. It lives it like a game collecting spiritual things and spiritual ideas. But one day, the seeker will notice a difference between this so called ego and its origin. Like noticing the strings on a marionette, or the prisoner who discovers the door was never locked. They realize that the ego is just a shadow of something far more eternal, and far more beautiful than the things we own, or the names we hold.

And it's at this moment, that the ego panics. Because it discovers in a very rude way that this path of enlightenment is actually suicide of the ego. This sutra refers to the point of no return. That when you venture far enough, all things reaffirm this truth. A screaming child, a discarded newspaper, a running faucet. Even in the most mundane experiences, the world proves how much more beautiful and real it is than our short-lived lifetime, and our short-lived desires. And it will do so by everything perceived.

Everything will show us the way home.

Text 4.27

तच्छिद्रेषु प्रत्ययान्तराणि संस्कारेभ्यः
tac-chidreṣu pratyaya-antarāṇi saṁskārebhyaḥ

tat	This
cidrreṣu	Break, breach
pratyayān	Ideas
antaraṇi	Other
saṁskārebhyaḥ	Preconceptions, subliminal impressions

Even enlightenment is broken up by deep conscious imprints.

At the zenith of absolute awareness, there is no self, no consciousness, no lover or loved. Only union. But even this state is broken up by our latent conscious imprints. Even in our best meditation, our identity comes knocking on our door.

But this experience should be completely welcome. We should never deny ourselves the experience of being, even when being means being under illusion. The difference between being under illusion and being under illusion is the context of your state of mind. Are you aware that you're not being yourself while you are experiencing another self?

There is a very real cognitive muscle that is being trained in meditation, but it's not focus. Focus is the side effect. What you're really training is your ability to return.

To recognize you've been led astray, and to return to your practice. You eventually get so talented at this returning, that even in the most hallucinogenic dream, you can find yourself again. And so breath by breath we develop the art of returning. Wading through the broken ice of our conscious imprints having a greater context of our perception.

Text 4.28

हानमेषां क्लेशवदुक्तम्
hānam-eṣāṁ kleśavad-uktam

hānam	Removal
eṣām	Of them
kleśa	Afflictions
kleśavad	Like the kleśas
uktam	Is said

Removing conscious imprints works the same as removing assumptions.

Experience writes conscious imprints. And those imprints manifest through the entirety of our personality and perception. The beginner begins the process of yoga by first letting go of their assumptions.

They embrace uncertainty, and accept a world they no longer have to understand. They do this until the world can, for the first time in their life, just be itself. That is, without their opinions and anxieties, the people around them can simply be themselves. Eventually, the student will start catching glimpses of what a broader context of life can be.

There will be moments when they'll notice how it feels to be emotionally and mentally free. But they will keep falling back into their anxieties and fears. So the advanced student goes deeper. Eventually, they will reach out to resolve the origin of their perception, their deepest subconscious imprints so they can remain in a state of pure emotional and mental freedom indefinitely.

In the previous sutra, we discussed the art of returning. But what causes the return? All around us, there are infinite threads of thought. Threads that have lead generations of us to build empires of patterns. A thought comes to us, and like a dog to a bread crumb, we chase after it. Sometimes for the rest of our life. That is, unless by some miracle, we make the choice to return. To return to our truth, a state of perfect restfulness. And when we do that, we leave behind a bookmark.

Confront the same phenomenon again, and we find that same bookmark again, and we return again. At first our bookmarks are obvious. They may be incense, devotional music, or the reminder to offer your food before we eat. For the advanced student, existence is the reminder. And they are in a perpetual state of return.

Text 4.29

प्रसंख्यानेऽप्यकुसीदस्य सर्वथा विवेकख्यातेः
धर्ममेघस्समाधिः

prasaṁkhyāne-'py-akusīdasya sarvathā vivekakhyāteḥ
dharma-meghas-samādhiḥ

prasaṁkhyāne	Meditative wisdom
api	Even
akusīdasya	Having no interest
sarvathā	Entirely
viveka	Discernment
khyāti	Insight
dharma	Nature, function
meghaḥ	Cloud
samādhiḥ	Meditative absorption

When we see the difference between knowing anything and Truth, losing interest in so-called knowledge, rain clouds of virtue and eternal consciousness follow.

Carefully we set aside what is real and unreal. It becomes easier to tell the difference, the broader our context of life. If the context of our life is just this very brief lifetime, we'll never tell the difference. But if our context is our legacy, suddenly the difference is illuminated.

Now the context of our life isn't just our single short life, but it's all of our lives. Not just our success, but the entirety of nature. Not just what we see, but what it actually is. And we look back at our self, and we realize — that every single drop of water, every passing cloud, or any other person that ever dreamed was apart of the same entity. The same being — just being.

The context of life becomes so broad that the simple statement of I am could never be said without including all of life and all of everyone. Eventually, we arrive at a point where even knowing is superficial. In context of pure awareness, knowing becomes synonymous with lying. And so we set aside knowledge as unreal. Our context broadens even more. And the clouds of eternal consciousness open up.

Text 4.30

ततः क्लेशकर्मनिवृत्तिः
tataḥ kleśa-karma-nivṛttiḥ

tataḥ	From there
kleśa	Afflictions
karma	Physics, cause and effect
nivṛttiḥ	Cessation

Thereafter, impurities in the conscious and subconscious, and all outward effects cease to exist.

Rarely, if ever, do we make choices. Going to the store, watching a movie, choosing a workout regime, pursuing a career — none of these are actual choices. If you put a rat between two trays; one with cheese, and the other empty. The rat will go for the one with cheese.

And you could by all means say, it chose the cheese, but there was nothing conscious about it. It was simple mechanics. The body needed to survive. A very simple chemical process occurred. The rat reacted.

Human expression and reaction is a bit more elaborate. But it is, nonetheless, extremely easy to quantify, shepherd, and for the 1%, — profiteer from. Humans rarely, if ever, actually make their own choices. They simply react. And the reason why they do so is because the context of their choices do not begin at a ground zero. Not at pure awareness, or presence, or lets just call it reality.

Instead, their context begins somewhere far off to the left or right. It begins usually with need, or an elaborate phantasmagoria of desire. And so these are not choices. They are reactions. Just like a drop of water in a river isn't making a choice to move. Just like people don't choose to vote in elections. They are manufactured to react.

But all of this is spoiled by conscious awareness. When we uncover enlightenment — our internal and external cause and effect cease to exist — we completely sever the umbilical cord of the world that brought us to this moment. We no longer react. We see. And we act. This is the only time an actual choice can happen. Otherwise, everything else is just coincidence and programming. Decisions that are manufactured by frequency times reach.

Text 4.31

तदा सर्वावरणमलापेतस्य ज्ञानस्यानन्त्यात् ज्ञेयमल्पम्

tadā sarva-āvaraṇa-malāpetasya jñānasya-ānantyāt jñeyamalpam

tadā	From this
sarva	All
āvaraṇa	Veil, covering
mala	Impurities, imperfections
apetasya	Removed
jñānasya	Of knowledge
ānanta	Infinity
ānantayāt	Because of infinity
jñeya	That which is real
alpam	Little

And so, when every veil of abstraction is removed, you realize that because knowledge is unlimited — there is very little to know.

When you love without reason, you live without borders. For most of us though, love only comes at the approval of some kind of imaginary consequence. Some kind of imagined reason. We tell ourselves, I can only be happy when so and so occurs. And only then and then only! And this mindset gets worse over time.

Because the longer we wait to be accepted by our imaginary standards, the harder they get to reach. The more we get hurt, the harder they get to reach. Until our imaginary standards get so high, that the very notion of being happy becomes completely codependent on being someone or doing something or buying something that you don't have yet (and let's be honest, it's always someone you will never be, something you will never have, and something you could never afford).

But love is so simple. It doesn't even require a lover or a loved. It doesn't need reason or consequence. In the most mundane place at the most insignificant time, your deepest and most comforting sense of happiness is right there waiting for you. The only thing stopping you is you. You don't need a reason to feel complete and at peace.

In this sutra, Patanjali disregards the knowledge required to realize this. What needs to be known until the heart is full of love? And when the heart is full of love, what else is there to be known?

Text 4.32

ततः कृतार्थानं परिणामक्रमसमाप्तिर्गुणानाम्
tataḥ kṛtārthānaṁ pariṇāma-krama-samāptir-guṇānām

tataḥ	From that
kṛta	Accomplished
arthāna	Goal, purpose
pariṇāma	Change, development
krama	Sequence
parisamāptir	Cessation
guṇānām	All matter, three basic qualities

From this, the varied threads of quality and change have fulfilled their purpose and come to an end.

We are the universe experiencing itself. From the very beginning there was only void. And in its exhalation, a myriad of stars were strewn across the heavens. We reenact this genesis of the cosmos in every breath.

Sit there long enough, and our imagination curls and wavers around us like a fragrance. From nothing, a myriad of perception is born. And then we inhale. The multiverse contracts. And once again there is void.

Once again, we discover a reasonless presence. Existence beyond description. Beyond self. Back and forth. Inhale. Exhale. Like waves reckless across the shore.

Coming into contact with God-consciousness means raising the context of our perception above the inhalation and exhalation. Its a context so high that from it, your body, life, and name are irrelevant. The only thing left is awareness. Not your awareness. Just awareness. And from here, ebb and flow of all time can be seen.

Tension and release. Inhale and exhale. First there are mountains. Then there are no mountains. From this perspective, you come to realize that the material world's, and its infinite manifestations, were only there remind you to return — to return to the one.

Text 4.33

क्षणप्रतियोगी परिणामापरान्त निर्ग्राह्यः क्रमः

kṣaṇa-pratiyogī pariṇāma-aparānta nirgrāhyaḥ kramaḥ

kṣaṇa	Moment
pratiyogī	Uninterrupted succession
pariṇāma	Change
aparānta	Death, end
nirgrāhyaḥ	Perceivable
kramaḥ	Sequence, progression

The uninterrupted flow of time can be understood by a myriad of reference points. But only when we let these references go can we exist at the fountainhead of presence.

The very best of travelers have no plans. They're not interested in where they've come from. Nor are they interested in where they're going. They are the easiest to amuse. And generally travel the furthest, and see more of the life we share than any other human being that is shackled by their time or agenda.

Efficiency! you might argue is only possible by a strict sense of time. In a material sense, yes. You're correct. But happiness isn't regulated by our efficiency. It's actually the fruit of simply letting go. Letting go of our work, letting go of the self, and ultimately letting go of our time. Living for no reason but to just live. Allowing ourselves to be happy for no reason but to just be happy. That sense of peace is your birthright.

Text 4.34

पुरुषार्थशून्यानां गुणानांप्रतिप्रसवः कैवल्यं स्वरूपप्रतिष्ठा वा चितिशक्तिरिति

puruṣa-artha-śūnyānāṁ guṇānāṁ-pratiprasavaḥ
kaivalyaṁ svarūpa-pratiṣṭhā vā citiśaktiriti

puruṣa	Eternal truth
artha	Goal
śūnyānām	Devoid of
guṇānām	Of the guṇās
pratiprasavaḥ	Return to original state
kaivalyam	Pure liberation,
svarūpa	enlightenment
pratiṣṭhā	Own form
vā	Situated, established
citi-śaktiḥ	Or
iti	Power of consciousness
	Thus, the end

The purpose of pure awareness is to be unobscured by quality. To return, all alone, to essential nature. The end.

To experience presence, you must let go of everything. Everything that will ever be. Everything that ever was. But even then, we only catch a glimpse of this so called fleeting presence.

We carry decades of programmed habits, patterns, and a myriad of psychological nuances designed to chase after an illusive carrot held just out of reach. For some of us, the carrot is the most important thing; call it a career, or a name, or very simply a life.

But of anything we can chase after in life, nothing has importance without context. And the greater the goal, the greater the context that individual has. And so if the greatest context is eternal love, then the greatest goal would be to just notice it. Which is, in all fairness, more difficult than acquiring all the wealth and prestige in the world.

No accomplishment parallels the means of letting go and simply just being. And so, my fellow traveler, if we choose to go deeper and discover this presence — we must go alone. No one can come with us. No philosophy, religion, or practice can take us there. Not even this body. And though there may still be a body that speaks and dances and loves. It is no longer yours. Because who you are, who you really are — is the grace among us all.